Business Planning for Editorial Freelancers:

A Guide for New Starters

Louise Harnby

in association with
The Publishing Training Centre

ISBN-13: 978-1484106211

ISBN-10: 1484106210

RECENT REVIEWS

This is exactly the book that would-be editorial freelancers need to read before setting up their businesses. Author Louise Harnby gives practical, straightforward business advice and backs it up with portraits of successful editorial professionals. The case studies are instructive and inspiring. I will highly recommend Business Planning for Editorial Freelancers *to all of the editors I mentor.*

Katharine O'Moore-Klopf, ELS; KOK Edit, USA

Louise Harnby's Business Planning for Editorial Freelancers *is a savvy and realistic guide to what, for new entrants, can be a difficult field to enter. Louise combines a business-first approach with a richly informative overview of the profession that will be invaluable to newbies. In addition, the 'practitioner focus' sections are an outstanding feature and enable the reader to learn from several other highly respected figures in the industry. If you're thinking of setting out on the journey to becoming a freelance editorial professional, make sure this is the first book you read.*

Hazel Harris, Wordstitch, UK

[...] invaluable to copyeditors who want to run their own businesses, and you can refer to it frequently as you build your empire. It will even teach something to those of us who have been freelancing for a while ... the book is well worth the investment to succeed with your new business.

Erin Brenner, Copyediting.com, USA

Everybody: if you want to be a freelancer, read this book. If you want to be an editor: read it. If you're well into your career and stuck – in need of a direction: read it. This guide will save you tons of time. It will help you shape the path you are on, so you get where you want to be.

Adrienne Mongomerie, Editing by Catch the Sun, Canada

This guide is essential reading for anyone thinking of setting themselves up as a freelance editor or, as Louise Harnby emphasizes throughout, an editorial business owner. With Top Tips and Learning Goals, every area of how to plan your new business is covered in practical terms, backed up by case studies of some of the industry's most successful freelance editors. For those new to publishing, as well as those moving into self-employment with a publishing background, this guide offers everything you need to know to get your business off the ground and moving in the right direction.

Jen Hamilton-Emery, Salt Publishing, UK

With this e-book, Louise Harnby has created a resource both interesting and useful for editorial freelancers embarking on their businesses. Helpful, hopeful, yet realistic about the challenges ahead, this book will leave its readers better informed, and therefore better prepared, for their entry into this highly competitive field. I feel sure that I can speak for production editors in other publishing houses too when I say that despite a well-populated database to choose from, a qualified, trusted freelance colleague is always sure to find themselves inundated with offers of work. Louise has, so far, declined to look into the possibility of cloning her professional self; this book is a valuable enough resource that I take the liberty of predicting that newer colleagues using it to chart their own trajectories will ensure that she does not need to.

Madhubanti Bhattacharyya, Edward Elgar Publishing, UK

I wish your book had been around when I started out with freelance editing. I especially appreciated the 'case studies'. I think freelancers who are starting out will be able to see themselves in some of those stories ... You've also given freelancers helpful action steps for building their businesses, and all of it in a highly readable package.

Corina Koch MacLeod, Beyond Paper Editing, Canada

ACKNOWLEDGEMENTS

My thanks to my colleagues and friends at SAGE Publications, from whom I learned the language of social science publishing; to the many freelance editors and proofreaders from all over the world who continue to provide me with professional support, friendship and unending wisdom; to the folk at The Publishing Training Centre for their enthusiastic backing of this project; to Kate Haigh, Liz Jones, Nick Jones, Janet MacMillan, Anna Sharman and Marcus Trower for their invaluable contributions; and to Mary McCauley, Johanna Robinson and Grace Wilson, the case-study contributors who shared their recent start-up stories with such honesty and clarity.

ABOUT THE AUTHOR

Louise Harnby owns an editorial business specializing in proofreading for academic and trade publishers. She has worked in the publishing industry for over twenty years, initially with Williams & Wilkins and then for SAGE Publications. The birth of her child and the resulting desire for more flexible working arrangements led her to set up her own company in 2005.

Louise completed The Publishing Training Centre's Basic Proofreading by Distance Learning course with distinction in 2006 and is now an advanced member of the Society for Editors and Proofreaders. As of April 2013, she has over 300 proofreading projects under her belt.

She is the owner and curator of the Proofreader's Parlour, a blog for editors and proofreaders, dedicated to providing information, advice, opinion, comment, resources, and knowledge-sharing related to the business of editorial freelancing.

She lives in the heart of the Norfolk Broads.

Louise Harnby | Proofreader
louiseharnbyproofreader.com

The Publishing Training Centre

The Publishing Training Centre is an educational charity dedicated to the pursuit of excellence in publishing. It grew from a small department at the Publishers Association more than thirty years ago and remains at the heart of the industry.

The PTC's courses are focused on providing specific learning outcomes that are designed to thoroughly prepare freelancers for the work they will be asked to do. All the tutors are practitioners first and foremost, which means that they bring their real-world experience with them to the courses they teach, enriching the experience for students and making the training more practical.

In addition to its distance learning programmes, The Publishing Training Centre also offers a full range of classroom-based courses covering all aspects of publishing.

Visit its website at www.train4publishing.co.uk for full details.

CONTENTS

INTRODUCTION

If you are considering setting up your own editorial freelance business, this guide is for you. It has been written for those with no publishing background or prior editorial experience – the completely new entrant to the field.

While there are many distinct functions to editorial freelancing – project management, indexing, rewriting, fact checking, language localization, translation, copywriting, editing and proofreading – for simplicity, this guide refers primarily to editing and proofreading, since they are two of the most common points of entry.

Creating a business plan before you do anything else will help you to make the right decisions. Too often I receive cries for help from people saying they've 'gone freelance' but desperately need to work out how to acquire clients, or they're wondering about what training is necessary to get them started. I firmly believe that these issues (and others) need to be addressed before you embark on your business, not after. If you're not convinced, let me share the words of one of the case study freelancers featured in Chapter 10: 'If I did it all over again, I'd do all the business planning and courses before … I was doing my editorial training, not after. I think this would have given me more confidence in the beginning and prepared me for the reality.'

This guide offers one way of thinking about the steps you need to take to build your editorial freelance business. Your business plan may look very different and that's absolutely fine; after all, people order their thoughts and ideas in different ways. The point, though, is to ask the necessary questions at the beginning, to focus your thoughts strategically, and to think about substantive ways in which you will get your business off the ground. There is too much competition out there to risk not doing so.

Business owner first, freelancer second

It's difficult to imagine a bank, venture capitalist or other financier agreeing to support a business start-up if there's no business plan. The information in the plan demonstrates that the business owner has researched their market, is qualified to offer the service(s) they're selling, has developed a set of realistic financial projections, and understands what tools and skills will be required. This information gives the financier confidence that the business owner knows what they are doing before any capital is invested. It helps them assess risk.

The good news is that setting up an editorial business is unlikely to require external assistance – you will be your own financier. This doesn't mean the approach should be any different, though. Instead, you need to have confidence in you; you need to do your own risk assessment.

Think about the business professionals you have contact with: the electrician, the plumber, the window cleaner. Perhaps you know someone who owns a publishing company, a shop, a mobile hairdressing business, or offers bookkeeping and accountancy services. Like you, they have decided to work for themselves. But do any of them refer to themselves as freelancers? To my knowledge, they don't. Creating a business plan puts your head in the space of business owner first and freelancer second.

Editorial freelancing and beyond

There's nothing wrong with the term 'freelance' as long as you are clear about what level of business acumen is required to run an editorial freelancing company, even if you are the only employee. It's not just an ability to make sound judgements and take the right decisions, but also about embedding a business culture in your way of thinking. If you don't think of yourself as a professional business owner first and foremost, you could be in danger of not acting like one. And if you don't act like one, why would anyone else think to treat you as one?

Being an editorial business owner is more than just a being a proofreader or copy-editor. Business owners take care of their own accounts; we have a solid understanding of the market in which we are competing and the methods we are going to use to get noticed in order to generate business leads and paid work; we do our own financial forecasting; we organize all of our training and continued professional development (CPD) to keep our skills up to date; and we take responsibility for our tax and National Insurance liabilities to ensure legal, healthcare and pension provisions are met.

In short, we are the owners, marketing directors, sales managers, web development officers, training coordinators, distribution managers, IT executives and financial controllers. And after all of that's sorted out, we do some proofreading, copy-editing, project managing or indexing, too!

Writing a business plan is therefore the way in which we prepare ourselves for the many hats we have to wear.

Structure of the guide

This guide is structured as follows:

- what a business plan is and why you should create one;

- the many worlds of editorial freelancing;

- getting yourself ready for market with training;

- client focus;

- getting experience;

- financial assessment;

- getting noticed – promotion;

- networking;

- the practicalities (hardware, software and tools for the job); and

- case studies: three relatively recent entrants to the field share their editorial business-building stories.

Each chapter begins with a task and a learning goal. These aim to focus your attention on the actions you need to take and the desired outcome. Additional features include:

Practitioner Focus: real-world examples that enable you to see how practising editorial freelancers have applied the learning goals discussed.

Top Tips: useful ideas, resources and tools for you to consider when planning your business.

Key Points: provided at the end of each chapter to highlight core messages for you to consider at planning stage.

Resources: lists of organizations, social media networks, tools, books, online materials and training providers.

Meet the practitioners

In addition to sharing my own experiences, I've also drawn on those of some of my editorial friends/colleagues for the material in the Practitioner Focus boxes. Between us we have a range of educational and career backgrounds, and we specialize in a number of different client types and subject/genre specialisms.

Kate Haigh is the owner of Kateproof. With previous in-house experience managing production (including copy-editing and proofreading) of magazines, she started her freelance business specializing in proofreading for corporate clients, students and academics, though now works for a variety of publishers as well.

Louise Harnby is the owner of Louise Harnby | Proofreader. She specializes in proofreading for social science and humanities books for academic presses, and fiction and commercial non-fiction for trade publishers. Formerly a senior marketing manager at SAGE Publications, she has over twenty years' experience of working in publishing industry.

Top left to right: Kate Haigh. Louise Harnby and Liz Jones; centre right: Nick Jones; bottom left to right: Janet MacMillan, Anna Sharman and Marcus Trower.

Liz Jones owns Liz Jones Editorial Solutions. She has worked as an editor since 1998, and has been freelance since 2008, carrying out all kinds of editorial tasks from project management to proofreading. She specializes in non-fiction trade and educational publishing, with an emphasis on design-led titles, and also works for non-publishers.

Nick Jones owns Full Proof. He started out as an in-house proofreader for Yell in 2004 and built his own freelance business up in his spare time. He left Yell in 2010 to concentrate on Full Proof. He specializes in proofreading for academic and corporate clients. He also provides copywriting services to businesses.

Janet MacMillan is the owner of Janet MacMillan Wordsmith | Editor | Proofreader | Researcher. Having been a practising lawyer for twenty years she offers specialist legal editing services for publishers, law firms and academics. In addition, she specializes in editing and proofreading social sciences, humanities and business books, articles and conference papers for academic presses, researchers, NGOs and think tanks.

Anna Sharman owns Anna Sharman Editorial Services. She specializes in biomedical science journal papers, offering editing, proofreading and editorial consultancy for publishers and independent researchers. Following a PhD and postdoctoral research in developmental/evolutionary biology, she was a journal editor on three different journals before setting up her own business.

Marcus Trower is the owner of Marcus Trower Editorial. He specializes in editing genre fiction for independent authors and publishers, including 47North and Thomas & Mercer. Formerly he was a journalist, writing and sub-editing for magazines and national press.

1 WHAT IS A BUSINESS PLAN AND WHY SHOULD YOU CREATE ONE?

Any editorial freelancer who made a success of their business without some sort of initial business plan (1) was extremely lucky or (2) already had experience in the field and some ready-made contacts. I would put money on the second. If you are a new entrant to the field of freelance editorial work, developing a business plan is definitely sensible, and probably crucial.

A business plan is a document written by you that clearly outlines the tasks ahead, the objective/goal of each task, and some information about how you are going to achieve each one. It can be as detailed as you need it to be. It's also a dynamic tool – you can add to it as you complete each step or as you come up with new ideas and information.

Business planning isn't just about implementation; it's about consideration. By giving yourself the space to plan, you provide yourself with the opportunity to think about the different options available to you both now and in the future. Some of your ideas will be acted on, while others will be discarded as you embark upon your editorial freelancing journey. The decisions you make will reflect your business needs, your personal history and your personality.

Creating a business plan is something you do for yourself and for the future success of your business. Freelance editorial work is highly competitive, and you are more likely to succeed if you are clear about where you are going and what you need to do in order to get there. Your business plan forces you to think strategically about the field you are entering, who your target market is, what training and skills are needed, how long it may take you to build up your enterprise so that you have the amount of paid work you need, what resources are required, and how you will sell yourself.

In essence, a business plan is a like a roadmap – it allows you to explore and plot the various routes you can take to reach your destination.

The following statement from Lee McQueen, 2008 winner of *The Apprentice UK*, is often quoted, but I wholly endorse the philosophy and feel it encapsulates the aims of this guide:

'Business planning is important to making the right decisions for your business, whatever the size ... It shouldn't need to be complicated, but [it should] be effective so it can be followed and tweaked along the way – the fact is, if you fail to plan you plan to fail.'

2 THE MANY WORLDS OF EDITORIAL FREELANCING

> **Task:** decide which aspects of editorial freelancing you want to focus on.
>
> **Learning goal:** to ensure your further planning is targeted with the appropriate roles in mind.

2.1 Understanding the field

For convenience, I discuss editorial freelancing in terms of copy-editing and proofreading because these are two of the most common entry points. However, the field extends well beyond these functions: project management, indexing, substantive editing and rewriting, developmental editing, copywriting, fact checking, language localization, translation, manuscript assessment, editorial consultancy and document formatting are all aspects of editorial freelancing.

Investigate the differences between these roles if you are unsure of what they mean. Your national/regional editorial society will offer advice.

TOP TIP

The UK's Society for Editors and Proofreaders, for example, offers some sound guidance on the differences between copy-editing and proofreading in the FAQs section of their website. However, it's worth being aware that, particularly outside of the mainstream publishing industry, the line between the two roles can blur.

2.2 What's your focus?

Some freelancers offer all, some or only one of these roles. I am strictly a proofreader. Anna Sharman offers proofreading, editing, formatting, consultancy and assessment services. Liz Jones offers project management services in addition to proofreading and editing. Nick Jones includes copywriting in his portfolio. Which services you decide to offer will depend on your experience and interests.

- Perhaps you are intrigued by the intricacies of indexing, in which case you could build your business planning around this as well as, say, proofreading.

- If you like the idea of working more in-depth with a manuscript, over a longer period of time, and with regular and intensive author contact, you may be more suited to editing than proofreading.

- If you have a journalistic, writing or marketing background, you may be able to diversify your business by offering substantive editing, rewriting or copywriting services.

- If you are new to editorial freelancing but already run your own business in an unrelated field, or you've worked for a company where your key responsibilities included controlling multiple deliverables, you might want to explore offering project management services further down the line.

- If you have proficiencies with particular software packages (e.g., InDesign) you should consider incorporating these into the skill set you advertise.

Use your business plan to review your interests and skills and decide what you are going to focus on. This will determine your training requirements, client focus and market research.

2.3 Multi-skilling

Having a number of strings to your editorial bow can help you access multiple revenue sources. Take care not to run before you can walk, though. Substantive editing and project management are probably only advisable for the more experienced freelancer who knows their way around their core clients' business and understands how that section of the market operates. On the other hand, it would be foolish not to take advantage of an already-existing skill set. If, for example, you're confident in your writing ability, are fluent in a second language, or you have experience of delivering sharp, product-focused copy, then use the opportunity to expand your business remit accordingly.

To review some of the training opportunities for a range of editorial freelance roles, take a look at the Resources section at the end of the guide.

PRACTITIONER FOCUS

Marcus is an editor who specializes in working for independent fiction authors. Marcus refers to the service he offers as copy-editing and, for him, this includes a level of developmental work that others working in different subject areas might consider beyond a copy-editor's remit. So Marcus will attend to aspects of scene setting, characterization and point of view (POV) and flag any issues that are still apparent at copy-editing stage. His aim is to help writers consistently apply decisions they've made. For example, they may not realize that they've described all the characters physically in a scene except one. Or they may not realize that they've slipped into omniscient POV mode when they intended to be in third-person serial. This is in addition to addressing style, readability, spelling, grammar, punctuation and language usage.

Now take a look at a very different example that demonstrates how the levels of intervention carried out by two of our practitioners differ. Consider the different skill bases Marcus and I have, and how this affects the kinds of projects for which we would be fit for purpose.

PRACTITIONER FOCUS

Louise is a proofreader. For publisher clients this means providing a final quality check on the manuscript (usually typeset pages) to ensure that there is consistency and accuracy throughout in terms of spelling, grammar, punctuation and layout, according to her client's brief and within the context of a given house style. For these clients, extensive changes at this late stage of the production process are expensive. She therefore has to make judgements, according to brief, as to when to leave well alone. While for small projects (e.g., applications, short reports and letters) she does offer more invasive editing and rewriting services for independent, non-publisher clients, for larger book-size projects requiring more intervention, she chooses to refer clients on to specialist colleagues.

In the next case, we see how additional talents and appropriate training can be used to expand the service portfolio you offer.

PRACTITIONER FOCUS

Nick offers copywriting services in addition to his proofreading/editing work. Nick has a natural ability to write good copy (no easy skill) and he'd worked in sales for five years. This had helped him understand certain principles about selling (i.e. focusing on the benefits of a product or service rather than the features). Even so, he didn't make any assumptions when he started his editorial business; he honed his skills with a mentor to ensure they were top-notch. Copywriting now accounts for around ten per cent of Full Proof's business.

Now look at Anna, who has one of the broadest service portfolios in our practitioner group. Don't worry if you don't have her skill base – most freelancers don't! However, she's a super example of an editorial freelancer who has exploited her training, education, business experience and talent to the max.

PRACTITIONER FOCUS

In addition to editing and proofreading, Anna offers consultancy services for journal publishers. This involves manuscript assessment, commissioning review material and providing temporary staff cover. Anna's extensive publishing experience enables her to pick up production systems and in-house standards quickly. She uses this background to extend the breadth of her editorial services portfolio.

KEY POINTS

- Proofreading, copy-editing, substantive editing, structural editing, project management, indexing, copywriting and so on are very different skills. Make sure you understand the differences.

- Offering more than one type of service is a great way to maximize your appeal.

- If you are completely new to the field, it's advisable to stick to one or two core skills, rather than trying to be all things to all people.

- If you want to offer multiple services, make sure you're fit for purpose for each one.

3 GETTING YOURSELF READY FOR MARKET – TRAINING

Task: make a note in your business plan of what your training needs are, based on your potential client group, and who the key providers are.

Learning goal: to make you fit for purpose.

3.1 Why should you train?

Training is first and foremost for you. The appropriate training will ensure you have the confidence and skills to do the job – that you understand the method and structure of an editing or proofreading project. If you are completely new to the editorial production world, attempting to go freelance without the relevant skill set is not advisable. You may find yourself in at the deep end with no idea how to swim. Training is about ensuring you are fit for purpose.

TOP TIP

Being fit for purpose is essential because in the editorial freelancing world you are only as good as your last job. A new client will not give you repeat work if you fail to demonstrate your competence. Getting repeat work is, for many, key to building a sustainable business.

Secondly, training is a sign to potential clients that you have taken the time to learn the skills of your trade. Editing and proofreading are not just about finding spelling mistakes. Having a good command of language and grammar are only the most basic of requirements. Depending on who you are planning to work for you might also be required to use a particular markup language, understand publishing layout conventions, follow complex style guides, format references correctly, manage convoluted briefs, and understand when and when not to intervene. Additionally, you will probably need to be comfortable using a range of software.

TOP TIP

In case you missed it, let me repeat – editing and proofreading are not just about finding spelling and grammar mistakes. The skills you will need to impress a broad range of clients will extend well beyond this. Training is how you begin to prepare yourself for a much wider understanding of the editorial process.

Training alone won't automatically bring clients to your door – for that you need to promote yourself to an appropriate sector of the market and build your reputation. However, having some sort of relevant certification is an initial indication (though certainly not the only one) to the client that they won't have to hand-hold you and that you know how to mark up written material to a professional standard. And it will give you the confidence to practise your trade in the knowledge that you are fit for purpose.

3.2 What's on offer?

Everything, is the short answer. The options are numerous: distance learning and on-site; online and book-based; and DIY and professionally assessed. Some cost hundreds of pounds while other options cost less than the price of a family cinema outing. Googling for proofreading training courses throws up lots of information but little guidance on how to make a choice. Here are some ideas to get you thinking on the right track. The Resources section at the end of the guide lists a selection of UK training providers.

3.3 Is there a national or regional professional society you can contact?

This is probably the best place to start. Get in touch with your national editing/proofreading society and see what they recommend. Their membership base comprises people who were once in your position, so they will have some great advice to share, and at no cost. See the Resources section at the end of the guide for a list of national editorial societies.

3.4 What service(s) will you provide?

There are different levels of editorial intervention. Proofreading is not the same as editing (though the line between the two tends to blur when working for clients outside the publishing industry). Use your business-planning period to research the different functions of editorial production so that you understand the levels of intervention and what will be expected. This information will determine what course(s) you decide to take. Your national editing/proofreading association will provide guidance.

Different subjects/genres will require different skills. Structurally editing a science-fiction novel will involve a different knowledge base to that held by the editor working on an economics textbook. The challenges faced when proofreading a legal handbook are different to those when proofreading a recipe book or a student thesis.

3.5 What stage are you at in the process?

Are you definitely looking to become a professional proofreader/ editor or are you at the earlier stage of considering it as one of several options? If the latter, you might opt for a cheaper, preliminary short course to see if the work suits you before you invest a larger amount of money in a more time-consuming distance-learning course.

- An introductory course should give you the basics – teaching the standard markup symbols you need to be able to use if you work for, say, publishers and project management agencies; explaining the editorial language you'll come across; and providing you with an understanding of the various editorial functions (for example, proofreading, copy-editing and structural or developmental editing) and the differences between them.

- A more comprehensive course, say the distance-learning option, should do all of the above and much more besides: it may also include regular professional assessment, access to a personal tutor, discounts on society membership, access to student networking forums, and preparation for different types of project and a range of briefs.

- If you've recently completed some training you might want to consider a mentoring programme. Here an experienced colleague provides one-to-one training and work experience, perhaps on 'live' jobs but more usually on work that has already been completed. Contact your national editing and proofreading society for more details on mentoring opportunities in your own region.

TOP TIP

Think broadly – I advise choosing a training course that will give you the skills to work for a range of client types. This could necessitate a larger investment at the outset but will cover you further down the line. For example, publishers are a potential source of repeat work, so understanding their training requirements is a wise first move.

3.6 What are your potential clients' practical requirements?

Different client types have different practical requirements. The student sending you a PhD thesis will probably require you to edit or proofread directly into a program such as Word. The same may apply to a novelist or academic author with whom you are working independently. Publishers may require their proofreaders to deal with typeset page proofs, either paper or PDF versions. Or they may expect their editors to work within programs such as LaTeX.

This isn't the place to delve into digital workflows and file formats; rather, the point is to encourage you to think about the clients you will be targeting and the expectations they will have regarding your abilities. Use your business plan as a way of recording your findings as to what kinds of clients you hope to acquire work from, and what practical knowledge you need to have learned in order to provide a service for them.

TOP TIP

Don't make the mistake of thinking that the digital revolution renders paper dead. Fifty per cent of my publisher proofreading work still requires paper markup (though I'm supplied with PDFs for reference), a red pen and use of the BSI editing/proofreading symbols. Make sure you are clear on what your clients want and expect.

3.7 Assessed or not?

Assuming you've decided that an editorial freelancing career is the job for you, and you need a training course that is going to give you the confidence and readiness to do the job to a professional standard, find out whether your training provider offers an assessment element. I think it is crucial not only to learn how to 'do' proofreading and editing, but also to find out where your weaknesses are.

One of the most valuable things you can learn from an assessed course is not just what you're doing right, but what you're doing wrong. Problems that can arise for the novice who's had no one to critique their work include: over-zealous markup, under-zealous markup, failure to follow a brief even if this means leaving alone what you consider to be grammatical bugbears, untidy markup, and managing very different style guides according to client preference. Feedback from an experienced professional trainer is invaluable in this respect.

TOP TIP

Remember that old proverb, 'What the fool does in the end, the wise man does in the beginning'? It's best to iron out the creases while you are training, rather than make your clients unhappy further down the line. Recall the first tip given in this chapter – you are only as good as your last job, so alienating potential suppliers of repeat work is to be avoided at all costs.

3.8 Finding training providers

In the UK, we have the Society for Editors and Proofreaders and The Publishing Training Centre, both of which provide excellent training for editors and proofreaders – training that is recognized by the publishing industry as a whole. In 2012 I surveyed my own publisher client base and all but one identified these two providers as their top two preferences. One publisher went as far as saying that they would only consider new entrants with training from either of these organizations. However, there are other good options, too, that may better suit your needs depending on what stage you are at in the process and what client type you'll be targeting. If you live outside the UK, take a look at the list of international editing and proofreading societies in the Resources section. Locating your nearest association and seeking their guidance is a sensible first step. Fellow freelancers are also a great source of information.

TOP TIP

Think carefully about what you are being offered. If the training provider makes 'guarantees', such as the ability to secure work or earn 'fantastic' rates upon completion of their course, make sure you understand what's on offer. Gaining experience is always a good thing, as long as you are clear that acquiring one job (that may not be for the target client group that you're going to think about in Chapter 4) does not equate to an immediate and long-lasting income stream. As for rates, these vary drastically (see Chapter 6). Base your choice of training provider, first and foremost, on the quality of the course – the knowledge you will acquire and the skills you will learn – not on marketing straplines.

3.9 What else do you need to learn?

In addition to learning the conventions, language and markup symbols, you may also need to know how to use ancillary tools such as Track Changes in Word, commenting and/or stamps for PDF markup, or onscreen templates and style sheets.

3.10 What if I can't afford it?

I appreciate the fact that, for some, money will be an issue. But ask yourself the following: If you were setting up a business as a hairdresser, would you do so without finding the money to learn how to cut hair? If you were setting up a business as a tree surgeon, would you do so if you couldn't afford a chainsaw?

If you're still not convinced, think about this issue as if you were the client. Would you trust someone to treat your pet if they had no veterinary training? Do you expect your dentist to have the relevant qualifications when they ask you to open wide? New entrants to the field of editorial freelancing who have no publishing or editorial experience will be operating in a competitive market alongside colleagues who have years of experience, the relevant training and lots of contacts. Training can be expensive and this is exactly why doing your business planning at the outset is essential – it will give you the space to identify what your training needs are, the budget required, and the time to save up if money is tight.

PRACTITIONER FOCUS

Marcus has years of journalistic experience as a sub-editor and writer for national newspapers and magazines. He's also had a non-fiction book published. When he began the process of writing a second book, this time a crime novel, he realized he needed to learn new skills. Says Marcus, 'I subsequently took crime fiction writing classes to learn about things like POV, building tension, characterization, scene setting, dialogue mechanics, and so on. The courses I took gave me a knowledge base that is incredibly useful to me when it comes to editing the work of other authors writing crime fiction in particular and genre fiction in general.'

Marcus also studied developmental editing with the Seattle-based Author–Editor Clinic. 'I also did a course called The Business of Freelance Developmental Editing with them. It covered the nitty-gritty of putting together agreements, invoicing, etc. Everything I learned on that course also helps me conduct my business as a freelance copy-editor.'

3.11 What if I don't have the time?

Finding time to make yourself fit for purpose is just part of owning and running a business. It's not about learning for the sake of it, but about ensuring you have the knowledge and skills you need to build your company. Remember, time invested in learning is time invested in the future success of your business.

All training courses are not equal, not just because the knowledge base offered by the trainer varies, but also because freelancers' personalities vary. Some of us need more guidance and hand-holding in the training stages; others who are business savvy and have bags of confidence take a different path. The key is to consider your clients' requirements first and then do the self-reflection.

PRACTITIONER FOCUS

When Louise embarked on her freelance journey in 2005, she asked herself the following questions: What training is recognized by colleagues and potential clients in my region? What skills are required in my proposed market? What kind of course will I do? Her answers led her to The Publishing Training Centre's Proofreading by Distance Learning course. She wanted an intensive, assessment-based course run by a body known to the academic publishing industry – training that would cover her chosen industry's expectations and conventions regarding the editorial process.

Nick asked himself the same questions as Louise. The answers led him to choose book-based proofreading training based around Trevor Horwood's Freelance Proofreading and Copy-editing: A Guide, which includes some practice exercises. He also wanted to learn in his own time but was more focused on being able to meet the needs of non-publisher clients like students and businesses. Here the process would be more personal and driven by an individual's needs on a project-by-project basis, and Nick's choice of training reflected this. He came into freelancing with a strong sales and marketing background, in-house experience as a proofreader and a high level of business acumen. If, despite targeting the same fields as Nick, you are less confident and are an inexperienced marketeer, you may feel the need for more in-depth training.

KEY POINTS

- Training is about ensuring you are fit for purpose to build a sustainable bank of clients, some of whom will be able to offer you regular work.

- Research your market and find out what clients want and expect.

- Every training provider on the market will tell you that their course is the best, and they wouldn't be doing a good job of marketing themselves if they claimed otherwise. Asking the end users, however, is the key to ensuring you make the decision that best suits your business strategy.

- A quick phone call or a visit to potential clients' websites should enable you to establish the training needs for the market you are focusing on. If you can't find the information there, talk to fellow editorial freelancers.

- Don't invest in the cheapest training course; invest in the right training course – the one that's appropriate to your target market(s).

- Consider investing in the course that will enable you to work for the widest possible range of client types.

- Planning ahead will enable you to save up for the relevant training ahead of time.

4 CLIENT FOCUS

Task: make a note in your business plan about the different kinds of people/organizations you might target; consider this in light of your own experience, skill set and educational qualifications.

Learning goal: to give you a practice-based focus on the client base most likely to give you work.

4.1 Who are your potential clients?

Client types are wide ranging, but ask yourself this: are they all suitable for you and are you suitable for all of them? Freelance editors and proofreaders work for publishers, independent self-publishing authors, academic authors preparing articles for journal submission, students writing theses, pre-press project management agencies, businesses, magazines and newspapers, freelance writers and bloggers, website owners and professional associations. This list isn't exhaustive, but it gives you an idea.

4.2 What's your unique selling point (USP)?

In an interview on my blog, one of our featured practitioners, Marcus Trower, said: 'I think it's better to come across [...] as a specialist in a particular field than it is to sell yourself as a generalist.' I agree. Think about your background and specialist skills – your USPs. You are more likely to be of interest to potential clients for whom your background is relevant to the material they are publishing.

You may dream of editing crime fiction or salivate over the idea of proofreading the next Salman Rushdie novel, but if you have a degree in engineering you really would be better off, at the outset, targeting publishers, businesses and professional bodies with technical publications, or individual academics preparing to submit to technical journals. On the other hand, if you are fluent in another tongue, this skill could be a way of adding value to the editing services you offer to clients whose first language matches your second.

Specializing also makes it much easier to stand out in the search engines (an important consideration for anyone when doing a business plan). Getting to the top of Google for a phrase like 'academic proofreading' is so much easier than 'proofreading' because there is far less competition for those keywords.

Here are some other points to consider:

4.2.1 Educational background

If you have a scientific background, science, technical and medical (STM) publishers will be much more interested in you than me – indeed, most editors/proofreaders I know who are working in STM have scientific qualifications of some type. If you have a legal qualification, consider focusing on legal societies, law and criminology publishers, and law students. Publishers and independent researchers have told me how much they value their freelancers having knowledge of the subject matter in which they are publishing, so selling your educational background is a critical marketing tool and thus a key consideration at the business-planning stage.

PRACTITIONER FOCUS

In addition to her career background in social science publishing, Louise has a degree in politics. Her many years spent in higher education and in the office reading social science texts meant she understood the language, style and structure of the material. This knowledge base was her USP. It wouldn't make her attractive to a fiction-publishing client, so she based the client-focus section of her business plan around social science presses. She made a list of every academic publishing house in the UK, highlighting those with strong lists in the fields of politics and international relations.

Your educational background can really make a difference, and the more specialist your qualifications, the more able you are to stand out from the crowd. The higher your qualifications, the more you have to sell!

PRACTITIONER FOCUS

Anna completed a PhD and postdoctoral research in developmental/evolutionary biology and then worked as an in-house editor on several biology journals. Her specialist scientific knowledge is one of her USPs. She therefore decided to target scientific publishers and independent researchers planning to submit articles to biomedical journals. Anna's qualifications enable her to reach out to specialist sectors of the market that the broad base of the freelance community would not be able to access.

4.2.2 Past career

Your previous career experience is something you should give serious attention to when writing your business plan. Think about the skills you have and how you will present them in a way that demonstrates a match with your target client base. The aim is to build a list of clients who are publishing material in your field of expertise. Using your previous career as a marketing instrument will be vital in helping you to stand out from the crowd. The following examples illustrate the point:

- If you're targeting publishing clients, and you've worked in publishing, use your business plan to remind yourself that this is a key selling point. It shows that you understand the business of publishing: the importance of deadlines, the diplomacy involved in author liaison, the challenges that your in-house contacts will be facing, the standards required, the financial margins they are working within, and the broader editorial process.

- If you've been a social worker, you might initially target clients who are publishing in the areas of social work, social policy and administration.

- If you've been a teacher, consider targeting students, academics or educational publishers rather than trying to convince an independent literary fiction writer to give you a break.

- If you are an ex-accountant, consider clients who are publishing professional and academic material in the areas of business, finance, organization studies, marketing and administration.

- If you have an engineering background, you might think about publishers, professional trade associations, magazines and businesses in the engineering and construction fields.

PRACTITIONER FOCUS

Janet spent many years as a practising lawyer. Her USP is the specialist legal knowledge that enables her to go beyond knocking a particular piece of text into shape; her field expertise means she can help publishers, academics, PhD candidates, researchers and practising lawyers identify structural problems or errors on complex points of law that could have expensive consequences if left undetected.

USPs can be specific, as in the previous case with Janet, or more broadly conceived, as Kate demonstrates in the next study.

PRACTITIONER FOCUS

Kate had career-based knowledge of the business and finance world and experience of working in the public sector. Says Kate: 'I realized one of my USPs was the fact I'd worked outside of the publishing industry ... I felt that my experience would help me understand the needs of business clients and therefore help with my proofreading and editing of their files.'

4.3 Armchair specialisms and hobbies

Hobbies are not to be ignored – you may not be a professional photographer, artist, angler, historian or crafter, but a particular hobby may have made you an informal specialist in a field. There are many independent and niche publishers who will be happier turning their manuscripts over to you if you can demonstrate knowledge in a niche area.

One of my clients recently asked me if I felt comfortable taking on a proofread for a book about baking. I did a bit more digging to find out what was required and, realizing that I'd have no clue if teaspoon measurements had accidently turned into tablespoons, we mutually agreed that she would send the project elsewhere! What may be a simple home-based task to you might be a highly prized skill to a client. So, for example, if you're a mighty fine cook, then consider searching for those publishers with strong food and cookery lists.

The same goes for gardening, child-rearing, DIY or dress-making, just as a few more ideas. There are scores of books that are published in these fields so if you have skills in these areas, use your business plan to consider how you might present this as one of your USPs.

PRACTITIONER FOCUS

In addition to her in-house editing roles at several children's and educational publishers, Liz had worked for a packager specializing in art and craft titles. She is also an enthusiastic cook. Liz understood that this combination of her career experience and practical interests was one of her USPs. One of her specialisms is now copy-editing and project managing highly illustrated non-fiction craft and cookery books.

4.4 Do the research

There are no short cuts here, alas. Carrying out the detailed research for your business plan will enable you to reap the benefits when you begin your promotion strategy, so take the long view and do the hard graft. In your business plan, compile a list of all the clients you are going to contact. They should be relevant to your background and experience. Note the name of the organization, the types of material it publishes, and the name of the person to contact. Make a quick phone call if you don't know the name of the person in charge of commissioning editorial services. My initial list had over 70 entries.

TOP TIP

Think about what your potential clients want so that when you contact them you convey the right message. There's no point in telling them about how you can use the BSI markup symbols if they are a non-publishing

31

business that needs its editorial freelancers to work on Word documents. On the other hand, if you are contacting publishers who work primarily on paper, they'll want to know that you have this ability. So, research the client and find out the types of material they publish, the media they use, the services they require and the tools they'd want you to work with.

Take time to research each client, even if there are lots of them. Make a note in your business plan of their specialist areas so that you can customize your contact message. Round-robin letters are less likely to get you noticed than tailored ones.

KEY POINTS

- Client focus is about marrying your experience and skills with those of the people/organizations who are publishing printed or online material. Identify your own USPs in your business plan so that you can sell them on to clients further down the line.

- When starting out, don't waste valuable time targeting those for whom you are not going to stand out.

- Specialize first; diversify later. Once you have experience you may find that opportunities to widen your remit come your way, or you can actively investigate them. In the early days, though, focus on your specialist knowledge base.

- Use the business-planning phase to write a short pitch articulating why your client group needs you. Until this is clear in your own mind, you won't be able to convince anyone else.

5 GETTING EXPERIENCE

Task: make notes in your business plan about the tactics you will use to get some initial experience.

Learning goal: to give yourself practice, beef up your CV and generate those first testimonials.

Getting experience is the hardest part of the game, and it is more important when you're starting out than worrying about the price you're being paid.

Most clients want to take on editorial freelancers who can demonstrate that they know what they're doing. Having a blank CV and no referees won't make you an attractive prospect. Publishers, in particular, get hundreds of prospective letters every year from freelancers. They also have established banks of editors and proofreaders with whom you are in competition. Businesses are a different entity and may not be aware of the value of your services. Being able to show that you have some experience and that people are prepared to endorse your work will make them more likely to give you a break.

It's therefore worth spending some time bouncing around ideas and tactics for getting some hands-on experience.

5.1 Mentoring

Mentoring is an excellent way to gain experience under the wing of a practising editorial professional. Linzy Roussel Cotaya summarizes the value of mentoring in regard to the PR industry, but the point is just as applicable to editorial work: 'The mentor/ mentee relationship provides the newbie [with] exposure to skills beyond the textbook teaching to help that person fast track his or her career with advanced skills that will separate them from the piles of résumés for a job' ('Why Mentoring is Important to the PR Industry', Ragan's *PR Daily*).

Mentees may work on 'live' projects with their mentor, or on material that has already been edited or proofread but cleared of the markup. In the case of 'live' work, the mentee gets to experience the process of working under professional conditions but with the safety net of a tutor. In the case of completed projects, the mentee is able to compare their work with that of their tutor. Be sure to check with your mentor as to the terms and conditions around how you can 'sell on' this experience when you come to promoting yourself.

TOP TIP

Associates and members of the UK's Society for Editors and Proofreaders can apply for its mentoring scheme, though some previous initial training is required. Bear in mind that there is a waiting list so check their website in advance to ensure you meet the criteria. If you live outside the UK, check your national or regional editorial society's information board to see what's available in your region.

In the next Practitioner Focus study, Janet describes the process of the mentoring role she takes with the Editors' Association of Canada (EAC).

PRACTITIONER FOCUS

Janet, who is a member of the Editors' Association of Canada, as well as an associate of the UK's Society for Editors and Proofreaders, is a great believer in mentoring. She is a member of the Toronto branch of the EAC's mentoring committee and has been a mentor through that programme since its inception. In addition, she enjoys informally mentoring new editors in Canada and the UK. Her informal mentees come to her either by word-of-mouth referral or by asking her directly (usually already knowing her from one of the editing groups to which she belongs).

With formal EAC mentoring, it's up to each mentor what they do with their mentee. Janet adapts the process to fit the needs of each person. Initially, she asks the mentee for a CV and a list of questions and areas they want to cover during the mentorship. She often requires her mentees to carry out specific tasks on pieces of work she's already completed and then offers feedback on the quality of finished assignments. Later in the programme, for advanced mentees who have demonstrated high competency levels, she might, with a client's permission, subcontract a few live jobs to her student in order to give them genuine work experience. Janet checks the work carefully before it's returned to the client. In this way the mentee is able to get a feel for the pressures of real-life editorial work, but benefits from the safety net of knowing that a qualified professional is on hand through the process to offer guidance and evaluation.

5.2 Gratis work

Another method is to offer to carry out a few free pieces of work for your target client groups. For example:

- Small, independent publishers who can't afford to contract out work to freelance copy-editors/proofreaders are a useful avenue to explore in order to garner experience.

- You could offer to proofread a student thesis for free on a one-off basis by making contact with someone at your local university – perhaps via a competition.

- Is there a local/parish magazine that you could offer to edit for a set period of time, at no cost?

- Do you have friends who regularly write expansive business reports that you could offer to proofread?

- Might you search online for Google+ hangouts where aspiring authors look for help at a token price?

- Are there social networking sites that you can explore where you might pick up a few leads?

- Can you make contact with a local business and offer to do gratis work on their website or some printed reports?

- Is there a local charity whose aims you support and which might be grateful for some proofreading help?

PRACTITIONER FOCUS

When Louise started out, she did three pieces of gratis work for a couple of small, independent publishers. Her bank account didn't see a penny, but her CV looked a good deal stronger and she was able to acquire excellent references to sell on to prospective publisher clients. Indeed, one of Louise's now-paying clients has told her that he commissioned her on the basis of one of those testimonials. Some years on, one of the tiny independent presses for whom she'd done a couple of freebies grew rather larger. They still do most of their proofreading in-house but during busy times they've needed to contract out work. They call Louise, but now they pay her!

Some critics of this approach argue that doing a few pieces of free work for a tiny independent publisher or a student will affect your credibility. I don't agree – your future paying clients won't know you worked your backside off for nothing; they'll just see the work you've completed. Furthermore, those clients who offer free work do so because they can't afford editing services and usually have to do it themselves; those who can afford to pay do so because they want trained, experienced professionals. The lesson here is to get the experience from the former to make yourself attractive to the latter.

TOP TIP

Ignore the power of the testimonial at your peril. A good testimonial tells potential clients as much about your ability to deliver as a training course and membership card. It demonstrates that you can do the job you were commissioned for, in both theory and practice. Testimonials are ultimately about building a sense of trust with the customer.

Take a look at the following example to see how Nick uses the power of the testimonial.

PRACTITIONER FOCUS

Nick built up his business by advertising his services in Freeindex, a UK free ads directory. Go to freeindex.co.uk, put 'proofreader' into the search box and look at who comes out on top. Nick's business, Full Proof, has more reviews than any other proofreading service on the site, 133 at the time of writing. Full Proof is the business that visitors see before any other.

5.3 Getting out there and making your pitch

If you plan to work outside the publisher market, you could decide to just get yourself out there and make your pitch. This may be the most productive way in the case of clients for whom proofreaders and editors are not the first people that spring to mind when they are considering the presentation of their printed and online material. The business sector is an obvious example of this, so use your business plan to consider how that pitch might sound.

PRACTITIONER FOCUS

Kate decided the face-to-face approach was the best way forward in making those initial contacts with businesses, so she decided to get out there and pitch direct. 'I braved early-morning networking meetings, did my 60-second pitch, attended regularly and built relationships. For many businesses, having their documents proofread isn't something they've done before, so they're taking a gamble on paying a freelancer for something they often think they don't need.' Kate presented herself as 'one of them' – a fellow professional business owner and service provider with a skill set that would add value to her colleagues' enterprises.

KEY POINTS

- It's not about the money at the beginning – it's about planning how you will acquire experience in a particular field and a strong reference to sell on to other clients.

- Don't forget, when you come to executing this part of your business plan, to ask politely for a testimonial.

Don't be shy about this – it's perfectly acceptable business practice.

- At the planning stage, the aim is to draw up a working list of targets whose praise will speak to the sector of the market you want to focus on – the kind of people whose recommendations will be recognized by your future clients. So if you're thinking about targeting publishers, you want testimonials from the same; if you're planning on working with independent authors, then references from satisfied writers will work well.

6 FINANCIAL ASSESSMENT

Task: contact your tax office; then, with various timelines and client types in mind, investigate what your earnings, savings and liabilities might be.

Learning goal: to ensure you are realistic about the viability of your editorial business in your planned time frame.

Your business plan should include a financial assessment: what you need to earn, what you think you can earn realistically, and over what period. Bear in mind that it takes time to build up a portfolio of regular clients in a market where you will be competing with established and experienced colleagues. It took me two years to get to the point where I had a bank of regulars who ensured I was booked up six to eight weeks in advance.

6.1 Talk to your tax office

An essential first step at the business-planning stage is to get in touch with HMRC (or your national/regional tax office if you're outside the UK). In the first instance, visit hmrc.gov.uk/startingup. There's a huge amount of useful information available, including advice on how and when you need to tell HMRC that you have actually started self-employment, self-assessment, tax thresholds, National Insurance contributions and record keeping.

HMRC has kept up with the times! The website has links to free online webinars, e-learning tutorials and YouTube clips to guide you through the process. If you want to speak to a human being, call them. I found their advisors to be extremely helpful, reassuring and patient on the phone.

Understanding what your liabilities are at the business-planning stage will also enable you to start thinking about how to organize your accounts so that you don't get the shock of an unexpected lump-sum request from the tax office.

TOP TIP

Your tax office will tell you not only what your liabilities are but also what aspects of your editorial business you can offset (examples might include rates, heating, fuel, mileage, stationery, trade membership subscription fees, software, hardware, training and books). See the Resources section at the end of the guide for a link to HMRC's guidance on tax deduction for home workers.

Investigate a range of setting-aside options. You could choose a dedicated savings account that gives you the flexibility of instant access to your money, but that offers a reasonable rate of interest (quite a challenge in the current economic climate). You might also consider paying your tax office a set monthly amount via direct debit, thereby clearing your tax debt as you go. In the latter case, though, you've covered your liabilities but your money is sitting in the tax office's bank account.

TOP TIP

One of my favourite cases of how the freelancer can make their money work for them, while taking a financially responsible approach to their tax liabilities, is that of a colleague who invests a portion of her monthly earnings in the UK's National Savings & Investments Premium Bonds programme. She doesn't earn interest but has the chance to win tax-free prizes every month, ranging from £25 to the million-pound jackpot. She hasn't won the 'big one' yet, but my fingers are crossed for her!

6.2 Be realistic

There's no sure way of telling how quickly your work stream will start to flow, so be realistic about how long it will be before you are turning down work opportunities because you're so busy! I've seen too many online advertisements giving the impression that once you've bought X book or completed Y course, the work offers will pour into your email inbox. It's simply not true. As with any new business start-up – whether you're trading in baked beans, computer software, tree surgery or editorial services – it's hard work, it takes time and there's lots of competition. The harsh reality is that it will require a lot of graft, and the results won't come overnight, not by any stretch of the imagination.

6.3 Consider your personal situation

Your personal circumstances will determine your financial needs and therefore the financial viability of your editorial freelance business. Use your business plan to consider the following:

- If you are the primary wage earner in your family, your needs may be different to those of someone taking the same journey as you but who provides a second or top-up income.

- If you are in receipt of benefits it will be important to speak to your benefits officer to ensure that you will not be jeopardizing these critical sources of income until you are confident that you can bring in regular work. Make sure the officer understands the nature of editorial freelance work and the time it takes to build a regular income stream.

- If you secure work from clients who are in a position to offer you regular work (such as publishers and project management agencies) or if you have an established list of contacts that you can access with confidence, you may decide to be less conservative about future financial projections.

- Consider running your new business alongside your current job when you're starting out. That way you have a financial safety net during the client-building stage.

PRACTITIONER FOCUS

Nick worked in-house for Yell for six years. He built his freelance business up in his spare time, leaving Yell in 2010 to concentrate on Full Proof. This strategic way of thinking allowed him to plan and manage his editorial business at a pace that suited his particular financial commitments. By operating in this way, the growth of his company was driven by customer focus and market awareness rather than the pressures of monthly bank statements.

Louise's approach was different and based on her particular circumstances. She was on a formal career break, looking after her first child, when she embarked on her editorial freelancing journey. Her family had already adapted to living without her income. Like Nick, however, her situation meant that she set up her business in a non-pressurized environment, thus enabling her to plan strategically rather than with her finger hovering above a panic button.

6.4 What can you earn?

There is no straight answer to this. Your earning power may be determined by your client type – those with legal, technical or scientific editorial skills often have higher earning power than those working for trade publishers. Developmental editing may pay better than copy-editing, and copy-editing usually commands higher rates than proofreading. Business clients may pay better than publishers, students or independent authors. It will come down to the client's budget, and these vary hugely. However, as the example below from Liz demonstrates, there are no rules!

PRACTITIONER FOCUS

In Liz's experience, while the hourly rates publishers quote reflect the summary I outlined above as an approximate guideline, flat rates for proofreading can be more lucrative than extensive editing work in terms of how the hourly rate works out. However, she gives the following caveat: 'These kinds of jobs are shorter in terms of overall hours, so you have to do more of them.'

Liz's point demonstrates that it's not just about thinking about earning X or Y per hour. For many of us, it's the amount of cash in the bank at the end of the month that counts. Now consider Louise's experience in the proofreading market to see a more holistic approach to assessing the viability of different rates.

PRACTITIONER FOCUS

One of Louise's publisher clients pays £14 per hour for proofreading. They offer her one or two projects a month that regularly bring in a total income of around £600, payment of which always takes place within 30 days. Another non-publisher client pays her £9 per 1000 words, typically generating a rate of between £24 and £30 per hour. The projects for this client are much smaller and provide a total monthly income of around £20 to £70. Their payment terms are 60 days. The second client pays a better rate than the first, but the first plays a bigger part in the sustainability of Louise's proofreading business.

What the example above demonstrates is that whether a rate seems fair or acceptable may depend on factors beyond mere statistics. It's certainly worthwhile setting up a client/job-tracking spread sheet (see the Resources for a link to a free template) so that you can compare different projects over time, but I'd advise not getting too obsessed with the numbers. Instead, focus on the wider proposition; make choices based on what you feel comfortable with and on how projects contribute to the sustainability of your business in the longer term.

TOP TIP

There are various suggested and recommended minimum rates for editorial freelancing (for example, the NUJ and the SfEP offer UK guidance, while the EFA and the EAC suggest minimum rates for US and Canadian editorial freelancers, respectively). Don't be fooled into thinking that just because these rates are suggested, all client types will pay them.

Consider, too, the following:

- You may not be able to command high rates at the beginning of your freelancing career as you are still building your reputation.

- Publisher work doesn't always bring in the highest rates, but this has to be offset against the benefit of a potentially regular work stream.

- Many publishers set their own rates, whereas you can control the price when dealing with, say, students, businesses or independent authors.

- Some clients set fixed fees; others offer hourly rates. In the case of the former, your experience and confidence, along with any efficiency tools you use, will affect the speed at which you work and thus what you end up earning per hour. You might also be asked to quote on a per-page or per-word basis.

TOP TIP

Trawl the internet to see what other editorial freelancers are charging per word or per hour. Not everyone posts their rates online, but enough do to enable you to see the range of fees being offered.

Here are some examples of how our practitioners organize their fee structures based on the markets in which they specialize.

PRACTITIONER FOCUS

Marcus works with independent authors. His clients are primarily based in the US and he specializes in editing genre fiction. He controls the prices and posts per-word rates on his website. He chooses to be transparent about his pricing structure so that clients know exactly how much they are going to have to pay before they commission him.

Nick proofreads for students and businesses and charges per word. His rate for students is around twenty per cent cheaper than for businesses, but the students must pay up front. This helps avoid non-payment issues, improves cash flow and provides students with that all-important discount.

Kate, too, is accustomed to setting fees with her business clients, and enjoys the freedom of being able to adjust her rates as she sees fit within the more price-sensitive student market. Because of these adjustments she prefers not to advertise a specific rate structure and assesses the terms of her contracts on a project-by-project basis.

While Kate, Nick and Marcus take different approaches regarding publication of their rates scales, they all control what they charge. Compare this to Louise, who works in the main for publishers.

PRACTITIONER FOCUS

Louise proofreads primarily for social science and trade publishers. In most cases the clients determine the price. Some publishers offer a rate per hour and a budgeted number of hours she must not exceed; others offer a fixed fee for the job. It is not unusual for the hourly rate offered to be several pounds below the suggested minimum rates issued by the Society for Editors and Proofreaders. Because of her target client base, Louise chooses not to advertise particular rates on her website, but rather to discuss rates with individual publishers.

Set-up costs

Set-up costs for editorial freelancing are lower than for many businesses, but you'll still need desk space, a comfortable chair, a computer, a phone, an internet connection, various reference books (online or in print), appropriate stationery, relevant software for working on Word files and PDFs and a website. Some of the tools you need are freely available, some are relatively cheap and some (like hardware) are comparatively expensive. Some you will already own; others you will need to buy. Use your business plan to start listing what you've got and what you need so that you can budget for any expenditure.

6.6 Saving money

Because you are doing your planning at the outset you'll have the time to investigate money-saving options, thus enabling you to avoid unnecessary expenses. The following are just a few ideas you might like to consider.

6.6.1 PDF-editing software

Many of us use the free PDF readers available on the market, but some of us want the higher spec that comes with the paid-for (pro) versions. Acrobat is the market-leading brand, but for the purposes of proofreading or editing PDFs you can get the same functionality with alternative products at a fraction of the price.

TOP TIP

I use Tracker Software's excellent PDF-XChange Viewer Pro, following the recommendation of several SfEP colleagues. This is around one-fifth of the price of Acrobat Pro. (Note: if you're a Mac user you'll need to be running conversion software, such as Parallels or VMware Fusion, to use XChange.)

6.6.2 Online dictionaries and reference resources

Check with your local/regional library system to see what freebies are on offer. For example, the UK library system has a deal with Oxford University Press, enabling free access to Oxford Dictionaries Pro. This gives you online access to a range of OUP's excellent dictionaries, thesauri, *New Hart's Rules, Garner's Modern American Usage, Garner's Dictionary of Legal Usage, New Oxford Dictionary for Writers and Editors (ODWE), New Oxford Dictionary for Scientific Writers and Editors (ODSWE)* and *Pocket Fowler's Modern English Usage.* Contact your library for more information. My own library system in Norfolk offers a range of additional online resources that are free at the point of delivery but that I'd not realized I had access to. These are funded by my local authority through taxpayers' contributions so it's good to know I'm making the most of them.

Merriam-Webster Online is another excellent resource. The online version is based on the eleventh edition of *Merriam-Webster's Collegiate Dictionary*, one of the most popular college resources in the USA.

6.6.3 Efficiency tools – macros and add-ins

There are some fabulous free editing and proofreading tools available. Some are not free but still offer great value for money, not only because they are reasonably inexpensive to purchase but also because of the time they save the freelancer, thus enabling them to improve their hourly rate. Two of my favourite paid-for tools are ReferenceChecker and PerfectIt, both of which come in at under £50 for the standard versions. Editors Rich Adin in the US and Paul Beverley in the UK have both created suites of Word macros to help editorial professionals work more efficiently. See the Resources section at the end of the book for more information.

6.6.4 Software upgrades

If you want to upgrade, say, MS Office, research what offers you might qualify for. HotUKDeals is a super community-based website where users share the latest online deals. Ask your colleagues what versions they are using and where they bought them. There are some fabulous deals to be had on legitimate software if you take the time to find them.

6.6.5 Hardware considerations

Adding on a large second monitor is a much cheaper option than upgrading your laptop or desktop computer, especially if you think you'll be doing a lot of work onscreen. For the purposes of onscreen proofreading and editing you can pick up a perfectly suitable 24-inch monitor for under £120. Not only will you have the benefits of a larger screen on which to work but you'll also be able to increase your efficiency by reducing the amount of toggling you do between programs. If you're looking for a new computer, make sure you've explored all the online deals first and asked colleagues if they know about any special offers available and what software/anti-virus protection is included.

Mac users will not like me for suggesting this but you could (and it's a tentative suggestion only!) consider buying a PC rather than a Mac if you are looking to buy a dedicated business computer or your old one has bitten the dust. PCs are much, much cheaper, and you won't have to deal with compatibility issues or fork out for conversion software.

6.6.6 Society and training deals

Consider what deals your national/regional editing and proofreading society is offering. Keep a look out for early-bird registration discounts on training courses, too. Your local chapter may also offer valuable informal training sessions covering technical and business-building elements of editorial freelancing, none of which will cost you anything more than the petrol to attend.

Societies are worth joining because your colleagues hold a wealth of experience regarding tools, resources and working methods.

TOP TIP

If you join the UK's Society for Editors and Proof-readers in January, you get fourteen months' membership for the price of twelve.

6.6.7 Free online learning resources

There are also free online learning tools that you might consider exploring – visit the online Hewlett-Packard Learning Center for one example of free classes related to the home office. Even if these give you only an introductory flavour they may indicate where the gaps in your knowledge are, thus enabling you to make strategic decisions about which professionally run courses you should invest in. Microsoft also provides a number of free video tutorials covering its most popular programs.

6.6.8 Savings through networking

Make the most of online professional networking through media such as Facebook, Twitter and LinkedIn. These are superb for connecting with like-minded professionals willing to share their knowledge freely through informal chat, blogging and organized discussion groups.

6.6.9 International money transfers

PayPal, or even your own bank, might not be giving you the best deal on exchange rates and international transfer fees. Ask your colleagues if they are using alternative payment options when working for international clients. An example is CurrencyFair, a peer-to-peer marketplace that offers savings on international transfers.

6.6.10 Website

You don't have to pay for a website – there are some great self-build options that are free to set up: WordPress and Weebly, for instance, offer pre-designed templates and the ability to customize, depending on whether you're a complete beginner or a pro.

KEY POINTS

- Realism and honesty are key. It's better to err on the side of pessimism when thinking about how long it will take you to develop a regular work stream and what the rates of pay might be, especially in the early days of your business – that way there won't be any shocks further down the line.

- Take advantage of special offers and deals on training and resources where you can.

- Search online – you may be surprised at what you can get for free.

- Invest wisely. Deals are great, but don't necessarily go for the cheapest – go for what you need in order to do the job. By planning ahead you can save up if money is tight.

- Don't forget your tax and National Insurance liabilities. Consider ways in which you might set aside money once you start earning so that you don't suffer the shock of lump-sum bills.

- Don't rush to give up your day job. Consider running your editorial business part time until you have an established work stream and client base.

- Take a holistic view to assessing clients and projects rather than obsessing over X rate per hour or Y rate per 1000 words. Focus on longer-run sustainability when evaluating fairness.

7 GETTING NOTICED – PROMOTION

Task: in your business plan, makes notes about the various ways in which you can contact and sell yourself to your clients.

Learning goal: to ready yourself for first contact with potential paying customers.

Once you have identified your training needs, your core client type and how you are going to get some experience and testimonials, you will be ready to think about how you will access your market, how you will present yourself, and any deals/offers you want to make. The strategies may be determined by your chosen client group. Some require you to be active; others are more passive forms of promotion.

7.1 Which method is best?

There are no wrongs or rights – just different approaches. Planning ahead gives you space to look at what others are doing, not just within the world of editorial freelancing, but in the broader small-business world. If someone tells you that X approach doesn't work and Y is the best way, stop and think before you follow blindly. Perhaps X didn't work for them because they didn't carry it out as well as you could. Perhaps you can write better cold letters, design a more enticing web home page or present a better directory listing. Or perhaps Y didn't work for them because they have a different USP to you. My advice is to use your business plan to develop ideas about what you can try (however banal, however outlandish) with a view to exploring a range of promotion tactics.

Read the Top Tip below for more about marketing as a process of exploration and the concept of testing.

TOP TIP

Good marketeers always test. This is the first thing I learned when I began my marketing career in publishing over twenty years ago. Business advisor and broadcaster Chris Cardell believes that 'marketing doesn't just involve testing – marketing is testing' ('Marketing = Testing', Cardell Media). Testing ensures that you don't get wrapped up in a mindset of believing there is only one way to do something – that only method X is correct. Use your business plan to consider trialling different promotion strategies, particularly those that cost you money. Set fixed time limits for how long each test will last. If you don't get the results you hoped for, consider this as something learned and move on to a different tactic.

All of our featured practitioners agree that word-of-mouth referral can be one of the most effective promotion tools an editorial freelancer can have. Doing a good job provides you with a great reputation. To the new starter, however, this may be some way down the road. While you're building your reputation there are other activities you can be getting on with to help you penetrate the market and start to build up your client base.

Even if you aren't ready to carry out all of the tactics discussed here, using your business-planning phase to consider future opportunities is a good use of time and will provide you with reminders of things you'd like to try once your business is more established.

Science, Love and

Revolution

David Lee Morgan

DEDICATION

to my big sister Bri

Science, Love and Revolution is the text of the poems from David Lee Morgan's hit show of the same name at the Edinburgh Fringe Festival, 2013.

Translations of this poetry text are available in various languages at www.davidword.com

Cover photo by Jon D Barker

CONTENTS

TIGER TALE

I had a dream where the tiger and I stood side by side
And the air was alive with the music of our beating hearts
This is my tiger, I said. Isn't she beautiful
Her teeth cut like diamonds, but they shine like stars
Then the tiger purred, the purr became a growl
The growl became a word, the time to dance is… now!

WORD

[primate animal sounds]

HAND!

hunh, ha, hey, ho
eh, ih, ah, ew
eee, ay, iy, oh
TOOL!

pah, buh, duh,
tig, ga, nuh,
kuh, juh, le,
suh, muh, chuh
r-r-r-r-r-ragh, zuh, vuh
FIRE!

[laughter]

WORD!

mother banana berry beetle grub yam
sister uncle brother father cousin kin clan

impala monkey cheetah catfish

bow and arrow hook and line

hunger death desire

dance dream moon wind

wolf enemy dog friend

animal-fur obsidian seashell

river lake ocean

barter boat wheel

sickle dam plough

millet rice maize

water-canal

goat horse cattle cow

priest king city wall

prison slave wife

road army empire

ritual sacrifice

planet alphabet tablet scroll

number circle triangle star

festival temple diamond gold

paper money poetry war

castle kingdom pilgrim pope

nativity communion jihad hijra

lord and lady serf and outlaw

carnival cathedral catapult crusade

compass telescope sextant astrolabe

buccaneer sugar-cane cotton-gin slave-trade

printing-press protest guillotine barricade

factory foundry model-t monopoly

gasoline caffeine telephone saxophone

black-hole rock 'n' roll blue-suede free-trade

concrete wall-street war-crime picket-line

colony corporation contraception insurrection

hospital popsicle methadone chromosome

pizzeria gonorrhea nagasaki hiroshima

penicillin television auschwitz crucifix

lipstick dayshift weblog gulag hot-dog kalashnikov

microchip paperclip spaceship cheese-dip

blood brain demon idea

mud angel reason ikea

love anger grief absolution

vaccination air-pollution

education evolution

inspiration revolution

danger freedom

building breeding

without a *we are*, there is no *i am*

the river was a god until we built a dam

EGYPT

Growing up out of the river
Out of the dark brown mud of an African rain
Growing up out of the river
Swimming in the centuries
Black Athena of the ancient world
Dancing in the triangle and the square
Pythagoras and astronomy
Moses and Deuteronomy
Papyrus and the hieroglyph
Tempting Plato to leave his cave
And question the universe
Swept over by the Hyksos,
Romans and Mohammedans
Christians and Napoleons, British
And the never ending battle
Of wind and river, sand and mud
Mother of the Mediterranean
The Red Sea, and the Aegean,
Bowed down under the centuries
The brown top of Africa
Surrounded by a new black mud
That is drowning Arabia in a sea of blood

And the wind beings rise up

Desert wind sweeping the continents

Shivering the spider web world of

Sky and Fox, BBC, Al Jazeera

Listen to the children

Growing up out of the river

Where the Nile delta sings

In the cotton field spring

In the spinning wheel whine

In the factory roar

In the millions who pour into Tahrir square

Chanting *"Baoo demana we Baoo Kalaweena"*

You have stolen our blood and kidneys

"We Bneshhat Ehna we Ahaleena"

We are the starving families

You have given our land to strangers

You have traded in lies and torture

You have dined on blood and murder

You live in palaces

Drive by us in limousines

Fly over us in jets

Rule over us as if we were nothing but slaves

Now we rise up from the grave

And you will do anything to stop us

Ballot boxes stuffed full of corpses

Rape and religion wedded to make monsters

And yes, you can kill us in millions

But how will you live then

Who will feed you

Who will dig your wells of water and oil

Who will build your chariots and palaces

Who will build your magnificent tombs

You will never defeat us

We carry the earth on our backs

We open our mouths and speak in flame

We lift up our eyes and see it is you who are afraid

We will bury you

And your bones will nourish our dreams

BULLET

(London, August 2011)

Bang! out of the barrel of a gun I sped
Into the body of a black man
Into the body of a black
BOY BOY BOY
Assume the position
Spread 'em wide
In front of your girl friend
In front of your mother
In front of your daughter and son
Put you in prison, yes, and I kill plenty
But even better, I make you into your own death penalty
I am the *War On Terror.* You are the enemy within
Man or woman, high or low.
Don't bother to show me your diploma
It's there on your skin

You are the flame of resistance
That I can never quite extinguish
You are the angry fire that I fear more
Than truth, and I am the definition of liar

You are the light that blazed up in Tottenham
And a hundred other places, so bright
It could be seen across the Mediterranean
I am the darkness waiting
You are the stand-up-straight of a new generation.
You are the broken glass and torn up pavement
You are the golden beach beneath, if only you can find it
I am the man on the TV calling you mindless

I watch you
Change into every color and race
Communicate in ways I can't keep up with
Be brave a thousand times in every hour
But look around – I still have power

I am the bullet and the gun. I am the serpent tongue
I move armies, empty bellies, turn bones to dust
I am a treasure chest of fantasy, pleasure and shame
I have access to your brain more often than you do
I'm running with you on your feet, it's my arm too
That torched your neighbour's shop, my fingers you
Must free from an iron grip around your thoughts
Kettling you, ghetto-ing you, four long days and nights
Letting you burn the wrong places, keeping you out of the right
Revolution is a hurricane and the wind blows wildly
When young lions roar in pain and strike out blindly
Jackals hide in the tall grass waiting their chance
Until you learn to fight with wisdom, I rule the dance

DUH-MOCKRACY

Back in the Middle Ages
They had this thing called
The Church
And it was their gig to tell you God's will and what to do about it
Then Martin Luther hit the nail on the head and said
You decide
But that was too simple and way too dangerous
So they backed off, made a few changes
And came up with this thing called
    Duh-mockracy!
Who decides
    Duh-mockracy!
Where God is the man with the TV stations
God is the man with the guns to take 'em
God is the man with the money to buy the guns to take the stations to con-
Vince the nation that he is the suppository of divine revelation
Who decides
    Well, we all took a vote and I voted against it, but…
Who decides
    Well, I don't like it but there's nothin' I can do about it…
Who put the lines on the maps that make the corpses fall on one side
While the other side plays

Duh-mockracy!

Who drew the lines around Palestine

Who dug a ditch around an oil field and called it Kuwait

They say there are no pacifists in gasoline lines, but

When the majority votes for national salvation

When the majority votes for mass incineration

When the majority votes for racial purification

Fuck 'em

THE AGE OF ENLIGHTENMENT

Je m'appelle Denis Diderot

They sentenced me to twenty-one years

Of frequent hunger and constant hard work

I thanked the judges and rolled up my sleeves

We were building a dictionary of the world

Covering everything related to human curiosity

So naturally we began sniffing at the asshole of the universe

Where the most beautiful flowers grow in shit

The sweet smell of stink, the love of calluses, rough hands

Dumb pleasures, howls of pain, life hungry death

Filth and excess, the word made flesh, and yet

Glowing inside, like a morning sunrise –

The rational mind

We collected everything, studied the work of every hand, documented every

skill, engaged the great minds of our continent, cast it all into movable type,

fired up printing presses day and night, shipped out books by the wagon

load, trailing mule shit and wheel ruts, crossing mountains, dodging floods.

We were an industry of the mind, making a new kind of product, selling it

to all kinds of people – not only priests and scholars – they drank us down

in the tea and coffee houses, and when they opened their mouths, our

words came out, but in a new blend, with the flavour of each new mind, and it bubbled over into the streets and alleys, palaces and dives, even just talking was intoxicating, as we all drank down the spirit of the times.

How could we be to blame for the holocaust to come, when we were fighting for the magic of the mind's wonders, for the freedom to ask any question? We were not an infection, not fanatics – we were the enemy of everything dogmatic – and revolution was not a religion, it was a clap of thunder, it was a prison break over the crumbling walls of a dying empire out into the wide open space. We were the liberators of the human race. How could we be to blame for napalm and the atom bomb, slavery, genocide, and a planet ripped wide open and gutted for profit and pleasure.

TIME OUT FOR DIALECTICS

We live in a metaphysical age

Physical, because even the invisible is material

Matter in motion, an infinite ocean of repetition and change

Meta-physical, because we never see it the way it is

We see it the way we make it to be

Which isn't to say it's make-believe

It's make-happen

And the happening is how we see

Until it becomes a habit and then it becomes how we don't see

Don't see the new

Don't even see the possibility of the new

But one divides into two

That's dialectics

For example…

May I borrow your chair?

Metaphysics says – the chair is there

I know it's there, because when I sit on it

(sits on it)

My ass doesn't hit the floor

Metaphysics says – the chair is there

Dialectics says – yes, it is there

On the other hand

(kicks chair across stage)

No it fucking isn't!

Everything divides into two

Because everything is coming and going

Atoms, electrons, ideas, emotions

Never entirely here or there but always kind of on the way

We look out at the world and see objects floating in space

But there is no truly empty space, and no absolutely indivisible object

Everything is process, movement and storm

One divides into two

The old and the new

The dying away and the fighting to be born

That's dialectics

BACK TO THE ENLIGHTENMENT

We were born into a world of circles, tied up in tradition, bowed down in
obligation to those who stood outside, above our circle, who were only ever
in a higher circle. I bow to you, you bow to him, he bows to the lord, the
lord bows to the king, and we all bow down to god or the devil, it doesn't

really matter which, because even hell is in circles.

And in a world like this, property was kind of democratic
Because it wasn't truly property until it could be taken away
By anybody – from anybody – the democracy of money

Property was individuality
Property broke down borders
Property was the atomic one
Multiplied by infinity
Property was possibility
Without property, there was no trade
No travel from country to country
Without property, there was no geography

And when we found that the products of the mind could be turned into property
Peasants who played violins for the lord and lady's pleasure
Became composers, makers of sheets of music that could be bought and sold
Even ideas became a new kind of gold
And what could you buy with it?
Freedom
The freedom of things
In the marketplace of ideas

There are those who argue
That true science and philosophy
Began with money

That the idea of a universal substance

Was not simply dreamed up

It was invented

Money became a fact

Then it became an idea

Only then did we ask

If anything can be measured in money

What is it that money measures

And so it began

The search for a universal glue

That would bind us together

But one divides into two

And if money is the measure

It must also be true

That anything can be broken into pieces

And counted

As property

Books

Property

Ideas

Property

Cows

Property

Loaves of bread

Property

Men

Property

Women

Property

We should have known
If anything can be measured in money
Property isn't ownership
It's being owned

BEAST MARKET

(*Capital*, chapters 1-4)

The Beast speaks

If I were alive
I would be your greatest lover
I would build you cities, feed your children
Fill up your lives with music and dancing
I would cover the earth with wheat fields and rice paddies
Drill down into its core to pull out strings of steel and oil
I would scrape the sky with desert sand melted into glass
Cool the hot, heat the cold, charm the fish out of the oceans
And teach the trees to stand in a row and rain down manna
I would multiply you

If I were alive
I would teach you the meaning of hell
I would blast you with war, rip your children from your arms
Swallow them in famine, smother them into silence
Dry up their tears with death
I would teach you to fear your neighbor
Train you to march in step

You might even come to believe in me

Isn't this how a wounded god would love?

With kindness and gifts, wonderful gifts

Mixed in with pieces of heartless cruelty

And if my cruelty is on a global scale

So are my gifts

And the greatest gift of all, I would do this through you

How else could it be? You made me. Now I make you

I am the law of value

The profit and loss ledger of the earth

I was born in the gulf between what you can do

And what you are worth

And look around

You can do miracles

But what are you worth...

How much do you eat

Do you live in a house or on the street

What does it take to make and replace you

That much, no one can take away from you

And still leave you

But after that, everything is fair game

After that, it becomes worthwhile to own a slave

After that, the more you make, the more there is to steal

Until you, who produce the food, become the meal

And the wonders you have made

Become a curse, become a plague

Become a gang of howling wolves

But somehow they are riding in sleighs

And it's you all pulling at the traces

And the whip cracks – that's me – I am the whip

But the wolves imagine they are in control and they

Snarl and slash at each other as they drive you forward

And you do go forward

So what if you leave behind a trail of blood

I am the hurricane that blows you through life

The profit drive, the whip of the world

I am measured in money but I am not money

I am in every good that goes to market but I am not physical

I am in every tool but I am not useful

I am you, your sweat, your time, your mind

Stolen away from you and congealed into a ghost

Not an evil spirit but an abstract principle

Coded into the grooves of habit and material

I weigh the world and say what is valuable

What counts

And it happens

Over an almost infinite number of individual transactions

I swallow and digest every exception, I break all regulation

I am the price of everything, I am the universal religion

I am the law

I am God

Kill me

Or I will own you forever

SANTA

Imagine you were this cool old guy who loved children
Truly and deeply
Loved every beat of the way they stiff-little-tick-tock walk, and the monkey
talk, and the roar of the buzz of the whisper of the butterfly why of honey
and wonder and thirsty hunger. They give you their hand with everything in
it, and your heart lurches into… Give me a place to stand and I will move
the universe, squeeze it down into the perfect toy to light the smile inside
your… I… would give you anything. Imagine this, multiplied by every
newborn smile in a heartbreak world – if you could be *Santa* for every boy
and girl. Imagine a magic workshop powered by twinkle of the eye drive,
quantum indecision, and reindeer jive, every elf in all eleven dimensions,
drugged and demented, but working with manic precision, a just-in-the-
nick-of-time engine (that's why they call you Saint Nick), and in the back of
the sleigh a bag big enough to carry its weight in wishes – this is it! the
delicious impossible minute when every child on the planet is given the one
perfect gift that says this is your world – and you belong in it
Imagine you could do this one wonderful thing
But for the rest of the year that was all you could do
And the toys would go out and be used up and worn out and broken
And that was good, the way it should be, that was why you would build
them
Toys were made to be broken, not children

But in the war-torn days of the in-between year, the names would change but it was always King Herod's reign, and his soldiers would go from door to door with bloody swords, while you all worked on through tears and horror, knowing you could never make it right, no matter how magical that one

perfect

night

What would you do?

Would you go on working

When you could only give the one magic minute

Better than nothing, and who could argue with arithmetic

Or would you go crazy with the weight of anger and grief

Would you feel responsible, would you feel like a thief

Living a life so sweet, full of hard work done well

When so many children are living in hell

Some people can't ever get enough

Give them a minute and they want eternity, the kind who can never be happy with even a scrap of cruelty, they go crazy at the thought of one child dying a needless death, they can't rest, they've got to be moving, doing, making more than a difference, making EVERYTHING different

These are the Crazy Santas who never give up

Crazy Santas mad with love

Crazy Santas get up at the crack of dawn, work boots on, march out onto the field, into the street, get beat, fight back, get shot at, don't stop, live life hot-wired

Crazy Santas are dangerous, but it's a dangerous world

Some people can't help fighting back whenever they see the weak attacked

They live like champions in the army of the never-had-a-chance

Some of them pick up the gun

Some of them live like saints

All of them are powered by love

All of them make mistakes

Some say we need more magic minutes that's the best we can do

But I believe we need to reach out for eternity we need to be

Crazy Santas who never give up

Crazy Santas mad with love

SAMSON

Did you ever wish you could be like Samson

Hair grown long again

Big and strong again

Between the pillars of

Right and wrong again

One mighty shove and then

Bring it all tumbling down

The end of a nightmare world

Where baby girls are put to death

For the crime of being the wrong sex

Where girls and boys are given guns instead of toys

And made to fight and die for the light

That's stolen from their eyes, cut to fit

And pasted on a Wall Street banker's diamond tie clip

Yeah, maybe the whip and the African slave ship

Have been replaced by the ticker tape and the microchip

And the factory sweatshop has sprouted legs

And learned to walk across borders

But every new world order it's the same old song

Where the rich have rights and the poor get wronged

And the chairman of the board and the drug lord

And the gun dealer and the born again politician faith healer

They're all singing in the same choir
Swinging and swaying at the same club
You get baptized in fire
They get their sins washed away
In oil and money and blood
Did you ever feel like Noah before the flood
Praying for the day some vengeful god
Would say – I've had enough
And wash those bastards away
Did you ever feel like Hercules
Sent out to slay the many-headed beast
But every time you chop off one head
Whack!
Two more grow back
Did you ever feel like you had so much love locked up inside
But you couldn't let it out, couldn't let it go
Had to keep hold of an icy cold silence
Or you might explode in mindless, raging violence

Living in a Marvel Comic Book strip
Knowing that the planet's in a death grip
Looking for a power that can shake it
Looking for a weapon that can break it
Look at all the love you got inside you
Let it be the fire that ignites you
Living in a world of violence
But the power is love and the weapon is…

Science…

Is dangerous, it

Brings on changes, and it

Opens up possibilities

Even the ground beneath our feet is

Not so solid, not so safe

They burned scientists at the stake

'Cause they were afraid of the trouble we'd make

And you know what? They were right

We can make day from night

We can turn darkness into light

And the power that reaches out to the stars

And into the atom and back in time

Can turn on a dime

And look at the lock on the prison bars

That keep us caged

It's a power that grows from age to age

From the work of the hand and the work of the brain

We think and we do and we dream and we make

And we learn from the lesson of every mistake

And all our achievements and all that is known

Are built on the bones of what's come before

It's true of the study of stones, stars, biology and human society

So when the powers that be sneer at our history

At our victory and defeat in the laboratory of the street

They not only steal from the living, they rob the dead

Of all that they fought and bled and died for

From the back alleys of Paris to the storming of the Winter Palace

From the cane fields of Haiti to the Vietnam rice paddy

From Tiananmen to Tahrir Square

From Malcolm to Marx, Mau Mau to Chairman Mao

These are our bones, our stepping stones to tomorrow

And the modern day vampires try to suck out the marrow

Of knowledge and vision and the courage that comes with them

But you who are fighting for a world that's not bought and sold

Where only in the human heart do you find the truest gold

You must be warriors with heads that are old

With wisdom and young with fire

Oh my sisters, oh my brothers

Don't believe the liars

WHAT IS TO BE DONE

the revolution will not come until it has pierced your heart

until every cruelty and injustice
no matter who it is done to
feels as if it were done to you
until you are naked, open wide
wounded by every homeless cry
a mother to every hungry child
a native son to every tribe
stranded in the forest flame
swallowing smoke and tears of rage
running from the thunder of a helicopter gun
the revolution will not come

until your back aches
and the sun bakes you
and the pain breaks you
until every minute of your life hurts
and the ripe fruit falls down into the dirt
because your fingers and your bones and your brain are numb
the revolution will not come

until every cop car is looking for you
for what you are, not what you do
and you stand on the earth, branded
by the wrong accent, the wrong colour skin
the wrong sexuality, the wrong mother tongue
too fat, too thin, too old, too young
the revolution will not come

until you walk the street, bearing unwanted seed
condemned to breed by men who call you girl
and think they fucking own the world
until you stare up into the hate-filled face of a rapist thrusting into you
when you can smell his breath, taste the rancid kiss
when your stomach twists in anger and disgust
when you can feel all this as if it were done to you
 – it's not enough

because the revolution will not come until it has made you wise

so what if you hate injustice
so what if you're willing to die to make a change
it's not enough to be brave, not even enough to love
unless love leads to wisdom, when push comes to shove

so you learn to read books and faces
you study what gender and race is
you look at science and the economy
at every class and group in society
you study the past but you don't live in it – you don't worship it
you don't pick through the rubble for a lost god to believe in
you read history not with a branding iron, but a blowtorch
you are not a king, you are not a priest
you are not singing in the fucking choir
you are the fire that burns through history
your genealogy is written in the ashes of
burnt-out villages, crucified slaves
weavers, chained to their looms
heretics, burned at the stake
screaming out the truth

how many thousands of years of fighting
each other over the never-enough, one
class after another rising to the top and
beating back down everyone else with
laws and religion and bullets when you don't listen
how many thousands of years of system after system

and always the same fundamental division

you work, they rule

but you are more than just a talking tool

let the revolution be your school

study the connections

and you begin to see the chains of slavery

are chains of power too

they connect you

to an army of the dispossessed

and it's an army you will need

power is a good thing
try living without it
but without a doubt it divides into two
the power to win is the power to lose
power is nothing but the power to choose
it's only as good as how you use it

but never forget
you are not begging for mercy
you are fighting for power

how will you break free of the ingrained habits of a lifetime
how will you gain control of your own minds
how will you bring it together to set off a chain reaction
and if you win
how will you fight off the armies that come to crush you
and if you win
how will you feed the world
and if you win
how will you carry through –
how will you free the world

be leaders who know how to be led
be teachers who know how to be taught
revolution is war – it has to be fought
they've got the guns and the weapons of mass communication
you've got the power to the people that comes with organization

you've got the power to the people

but you better believe they hate it

if you give 'em a chance they'll break it

you know it's only as good as you make it

you've got the power to the people

are you ready to take it

ABOUT THE AUTHOR

David Lee Morgan has travelled the world as a performance poet and street musician (saxophone). He has won many poetry slams, including the London and U.K. Slam Championships. He is a longstanding member of the Writers Guild and holds a PhD in Creative Writing from Newcastle University. He lives in London, grew up in the U.S., was born in Berlin and considers himself a citizen of the planet.

Made in the USA
San Bernardino, CA
05 January 2014

TOP TIP

Even the new entrant to the field can start to use the word-of-mouth strategy, so tell everyone what you do! Get some business cards designed and carry them with you at all times – just in case an opportunity arises.

7.2 Deciding on a business name – branding

You can use your own name or create a company title that reflects what you do. Whatever you choose, it is part of your brand, so be sure to make the right decision in the planning stages rather than having to make alterations when you're up and running. There are no rights or wrongs to selecting a business name, but some issues to consider include:

- Make sure no one else is trading under the same name. Full Proof is taken, as are Kateproof and Liz Jones Editorial Solutions!

- If you have an unusual last name, you may wish to capitalize on its originality and incorporate that into your business name, as I did.

- If you think you are likely to expand your service portfolio, you may decide to avoid terms such as 'proofreader' or 'editor' and opt instead for 'editorial' or 'editorial services', as Marcus and Anna did.

- Consider too how you will use your business name in your website's domain name. Including words like 'proofreader', 'editor' or 'editorial services' will give you a big advantage online as the search engines seem to favour keyword-rich domain names.

In the following example, Liz shares the decision-making process behind her choice of business name and how the result was determined by the message she wanted to communicate to her clients.

PRACTITIONER FOCUS

Liz's company is called Liz Jones Editorial Solutions. Initially, she had planned on the final word being 'Services' but changed her mind after attending an SfEP workshop on working with non-publishers. Says Liz: 'I wanted to capture more of a business vibe. I wanted the name of my company to reflect the fact that I can solve problems and present solutions, rather than just throw queries at my clients.'

If you are already known in the circles in which you plan to target your services, this might be a key driver behind your choice of business name, as was the case for Marcus.

PRACTITIONER FOCUS

Marcus has had a book published by a large mainstream publisher. Since his name is already 'out there' in publishing circles, it made sense for him to use the marketing capital he'd already earned and incorporate his name into his business title, hence Marcus Trower Editorial.

7.3 Presentation of core elements

Think also about how you are going to present yourself to make yourself attractive to prospective clients. Key features that you may wish to consider are:

- Your core specialisms/USPs: tell the client how your experience and background fit with their needs (their publishing list, their company reports, their dissertation subject matter, etc.). Try to avoid statements that indicate you'll consider anything. When using online media, core specialisms provide valuable keyword-search potential as well as enriching the content of your business message.

- The services you provide: e.g. project management, collation, indexing, proofreading, copy-editing, onscreen editing/proofreading, author liaison.

- The training you've undertaken: any relevant editorial training courses, mentoring schemes, accreditation programmes, CPD, society membership.

- Experience: a summary of relevant key projects already completed and the clients for whom you worked (even if the work was completed on a gratis basis).

- References: include a list of relevant testimonials from appropriate clients, or the contact information for these people (remember to get their permission first).

- Contact information: your phone number, address, URL, link to any professional directory entry.

TOP TIP

Focus on the positives, not on the negatives. I've seen websites and cover letters that tell potential clients not only what the freelancer's skills are, but also what they can't do (for example, 'I don't work weekends'; 'I don't offer copy-editing'; 'I'm planning to become a full-time proofreader when I've finished doing X'; 'I'd like to do Y once I have more experience'). These kinds of statements don't instil confidence in a client. Instead, recall the pitch that you've already developed in your business plan and keep to the message.

When you have a complete summary of the above, you can use this to develop and adapt the information to suit your website, covering letter/email, promotional brochure, directory listing, LinkedIn profile, Facebook business page, or Twitter sidebar.

TOP TIP

It's worth reiterating here the point made in Chapter 5 about the power of the testimonial. Testimonials engender a sense of trust and help clients to decide whether you are a safe pair of hands. Says sales coach, Liz Wendling: 'Trust is the single biggest motivator of buyer behavior and one of the key components to establishing a successful buyer/seller relationship' ('No Trust? No Sale!', The Sales Coach for Women). Using your business-planning stage to think about how you will acquire testimonials is time well invested.

7.4 The cold method – CV and covering letter

One of my preferred methods for accessing publishers and project management agencies is to send a cold letter. The term 'cold' is used because the client is not expecting you to contact them. I like to include a brief CV with my cover letter.

7.4.1 Why go direct?

I could wait in the hope that publishers find my entries in a couple of core UK freelance directories. Perhaps they might land on my website. Or maybe they might see my Twitter profile and think I'm interesting. Actually, I do promote my business using all of these tools, but I don't rely on them to get the attention of publisher clients. Why? Because in-house production staff are ridiculously busy.

In-house production editors don't necessarily have time to scout around the internet to find editorial freelancers. If I sit around waiting for them, I'll probably miss my chance – when they do find the time to search for new freelancers, they'll be too busy replying to the cold letters sent by my colleagues.

7.4.2 Something to keep on file

'What a lot we lost when we stopped writing letters. You can't reread a phone call' – I love this quote from Liz Carpenter (quoted in Wagner, *Cold Letters*). It sums up another benefit of sending a cold cover letter: the prospective client has something they can keep on file even if they don't have use for your services right now. Then, if those busy desk editors do embark on a recruitment drive, your details are already in their 'to consider' pile.

PRACTITIONER FOCUS

Janet, Liz and Louise consider cold letters/emails as one of their core strategies for contacting potential clients. They tailor these communications around how their skills fit with the recipient publishers' profiles, their industry experience, relevant training and the excellent references they can supply.

7.4.3 Think about timing

Try contacting publishing clients in the period leading up to the holiday season, as that's when their regular freelancers are more likely to be unavailable. This tactic means making sacrifices with regard to your leisure time: in the early days of your freelancing career this may mean a lot of evening work, but it will have paid off if you hang on to the clients. Later, you can turn down work if the timing doesn't suit you, comfortable in the knowledge that your clients value your work enough that you won't slip off their radar if you don't want to proofread on Christmas Eve.

PRACTITIONER FOCUS

Louise used the timing strategy when she was starting out. She posted a round of cold letters a month before the school summer vacation began. Two publishers responded with offers of work, and both commented that her application was timely, owing to their regular freelancers being on holiday. The strategy still works. In Christmas 2012 she picked up a new publisher client via the SfEP's Directory of Editorial Services, again because their regular suppliers were unavailable. All three of those clients continue to use her on a regular basis.

Timing isn't just about seasons and holidays. It can be far more precise. This is where networking with your colleagues can really come into play and where keeping your ear to the ground is an essential prerequisite for successful freelancing. If you're one of those people who thinks discussion groups and Twitter accounts are just 'messing around', read the next example from Liz and think again.

PRACTITIONER FOCUS

Liz has used quick-response timing to secure work she heard about via business networking. As she explains: 'My most regular non-publishing client came about because I got wind of the fact (via the SfEP discussion forum) that the company was looking for a proofreader, so I googled the person in question and within maybe half an hour had got the gig. I know others who have used the same tactic.' Your editorial society's discussion board, Facebook or the Twittersphere, combined with a no-dithering approach, could be key to exploiting new opportunities.

7.4.4 Focus your message

Use your business plan to build a profile that you can tailor for your cold letters, including the following points that my publisher clients agreed were key:

- Experience, especially experience of proofreading/copy-editing material in subjects that match the press's own list(s). That way they know you're familiar with the language of the books or journals they publish.

- References from their colleagues – publishing is a small world. People move around in this business and they meet each other at conferences and on training courses. X probably knows Y (or knows a colleague or friend of Y's). Being able to show X that Y values your work says something about your skills.

- Ability to follow the brief and the house style with minimum hand-holding. And if you have in-house experience, be sure to mention it.

- Deadline hitting – in-house production editors don't want sloppy time-keepers. Their publication schedules are often built around key events such as new academic semesters, conferences and book promotion tours, as well as seasonal holiday periods like Christmas and Chinese New Year, to give just a few examples.

- Competence as demonstrated by training/assessment – an industry-recognized course, criteria-based professional membership or willingness to take tests.

- Flexibility on formats – for some publishers, being able to work onscreen is essential.

7.5 Specialist directories and free listings

Use your business plan to record details of the core directories editorial freelancers are using in your region/country. For instance, in the UK, the Society for Editors and Proofreaders has an online, searchable Directory of Editorial Services. Publishers, project management agencies, students and independent authors can search by keyword for freelancers offering specific services in a wide range of subject areas. To see what other editorial freelancing directories are available around the world, take a look at the Resources section at the end of the guide.

Don't ignore free listings – depending on the client type you want to attract, they can be a fantastic resource that won't hurt your budget.

PRACTITIONER FOCUS

When Nick started out, he took advantage of a number of free directories including FreeIndex, which he describes as the jewel in his business's promotion crown. For Nick, not only did these generate business leads for him, but also they boosted Full Proof's search engine rankings because of the links he embedded in his profile. As mentioned earlier, Nick has used the power of the testimonial on his FreeIndex listing to maximum effect. With more reviews than any other proofreading business, visitors entering the keyword 'proofreader' will see Full Proof before they see anyone else.

Nick's choice of advertising was based on the results of his initial client focus assessment. My decision to target publishers led me to take a different route, as the next study shows.

PRACTITIONER FOCUS

For Louise, the two most productive specialist directories have been Find a Proofreader (owned by Nick) and the SfEP's Directory of Editorial Services. From the former she has been commissioned by students, business professionals and a magazine; from the latter she has acquired work from publishers, who have gone on to become long-term clients offering repeat work in a variety of academic subject areas. Some of Louise's UK publisher clients have told her that the SfEP's directory is their sole search tool for editorial freelancers. Entry in the SfEP's directory is restricted to members who meet set criteria in terms of training and experience; entry in Find a Proofreader is open to all and is excellent value for money.

Consider, too, moving beyond your own shores. As the next example reminds us, living in one country doesn't mean working only for clients in that country. There's nothing to stop you targeting clients from other countries, so use your business plan to think about what opportunities you might exploit abroad.

PRACTITIONER FOCUS

Marcus, who specializes in editing genre fiction for American writers, has an entry in the EFA directory. Entry is free but open only to members, and full membership costs $145 per year. The work he acquires from the listing ensures his investment is easily repaid.

Advertising in directories is a passive way of promoting your business. Sitting in a directory won't guarantee work, but if you're not in the key listings you certainly won't be found by potential clients who use them.

TOP TIP

Most specialized editorial directories aren't free so doing the research at business-planning stage will enable you to plan your investment wisely. By planning ahead, you will have the time to ask established freelancers which directories in your country/region they recommend in order to generate the kind of work you're interested in.

7.6 Working for others – language-editing agencies and other editorial businesses

Some editorial business owners bid on large contracts that will take some months to complete. They then subcontract sections of the work to other freelancers. Expanding your editorial network (especially via social media platforms) will increase the likelihood of you finding out which colleagues offer this kind of service and whether you might work for them. Accessing the market in this way is very much a word-of-mouth process.

More formally, editing agencies provide a way of bringing together editors and authors (usually scientific researchers writing pre-submission journal articles). In the journal publishing market particularly, much of the responsibility for copy-editing that used to be held in-house by desk editors has now been handed back to the individual researchers.

There are a number of key agencies that have links to their websites on the author-services pages of publisher websites. For a list of some of the agencies operating internationally, see the Resources section at the end of the guide.

PRACTITIONER FOCUS

As well as working for publishers, Anna also helps scientists preparing their articles for submission to scientific journals. One of her access points is editing agencies. She is educated to PhD level, and this and her postdoctoral work qualify her for inclusion in some of these agencies' editorial banks. Says Anna, 'Agencies can channel a steady stream of papers your way, from many authors, saving the time and effort needed for marketing your services to a lot of different universities and institutes.'

7.7 Meet-and-greets, workshops and events

If you plan to focus on independent writers, business owners and students, you should think seriously about active promotion approaches that put you face to face with potential clients. These might include, but are not limited to, business networking events, trade shows, workshops and site visits. This type of networking is unlikely to get you definite yes/no answers to your requests for editorial freelancing work. Instead, it's relationship-driven promotion that allows you to build a rapport with core client groups and show them how you can assist them.

PRACTITIONER FOCUS

Kate utilized the face-to-face approach when she realized that her USP was her own corporate experience. Rather than waiting for organizations to contact her, she attended local business events – often early-morning networking meetings – that put her in touch with entrepreneurs in her region. These experiences confirmed her belief that businesses aren't always aware of the benefits of hiring an editorial professional to look over their website, report or presentation. Once she told them what she did, they began to see how her services could add value to their practice.

Kate also made contact with her local university through the meet-and-greet method. 'I saw an advert for a networking event in my local area that was due to be held by someone who supervises Master's students and I contacted him to ask if I could chat to him before or after the event. He replied, we met for coffee, he took my business cards – as they say, the rest is history ... I think from that one coffee, I have had over fifteen enquiries from one section of one university.'

7.8 Personal website

I know many established editorial freelancers who don't have a website and feel they don't need one. They have a solid client base, built up over many years, and their reputations alone generate referrals. For the new entrant to the field, it's a different story. My own opinion is that you'd be daft not to have one. Here are seven reasons why:

1. **Competition:** proofreading and editing are competitive. If your colleagues have websites but you don't, you're less likely to be found by potential customers.

2. **No-cost promotion:** your website is a free marketing tool. If you use a host such as Weebly or WordPress, to name just two, then the only cost to you is the time you spend building and maintaining it. Once live, customers can find you rather than you always having to find them.

3. **Create an online résumé:** you can use your website as an online résumé. Keep your home page uncluttered, but use other pages to show off your clients, skills and portfolio of work.

4. **Control your space:** a website is more than 'having an online presence' – it's a professional space in which you control both the content and how it's presented.

5. **Content is always fresh:** websites are easy to update, meaning the content you include is always the latest content. If you update your site frequently, search engines are more likely to notice you. And that means clients are more likely to find you.

6. **It's not hard:** things have come on a long way in the past few years. Even if the idea of building your own site scares you, make the jump and at least do a bit of research. Many website providers offer design templates that you can use and adapt to suit your own needs. You don't need any technical knowledge of computer programming or coding to get up and running.

7. **Future-proofing:** my colleague Daniel Heuman, owner of Intelligent Editing, has some sage advice: 'When you're running a small business, things can change. You may find that a big client brings in new procedures, and suddenly you could find yourself in a dry spell for work ... you have the assurance of another line of marketing that's ready to go if things change' ('Building a Website for Your Freelance Business', Find a Proofreader).

TOP TIP

Include a picture of yourself on your website. For some, the idea of putting their face on the internet is ghastly. If that's how you feel, do it anyway. It makes you real to people. Anyone can copy a royalty-free image from the web and put it on their site, but there's only one you. Use the same picture for your Facebook page, your Twitter and LinkedIn profiles, and any other online directories or web spaces that you participate in. Consider it another part of your branding strategy – when the same picture is always attached to your business title, people will come to recognize your face in the same way they recognize your business name.

It goes without saying that the image you use should reflect the message you want to convey to potential clients, so make sure it's a professional-looking picture. My preference is for a head-and-shoulders shot, face towards the camera, and a smile.

If you've still to be convinced, take the advice of experienced project manager, Hazel Harris: 'Unsettling images may be off-putting, but an absent image is the first thing I notice about a profile. It gives an immediate impression of half-heartedness or incompleteness' ('Seven Ways to Make Your LinkedIn Profile More Appealing to Editorial Project Managers', Editing Mechanics).

Making sure your website works for both you and your readers is essential, so use the planning stage to ask colleagues and friends to preview your site, as Kate did in our next practitioner example.

PRACTITIONER FOCUS

Kate's website is self-built (with the help of a tech-savvy family member). For her, feedback was an essential part of the process. She asked friends, fellow editors and proofreaders, and her Publishing Training Centre tutor to evaluate her site and then tweaked accordingly. The evaluation didn't just concern the words and ensuring she'd eradicated any errors – she was also interested in knowing how the site 'worked' for visitors in terms of ease of use, navigation and clarity of message.

7.9 Blogging

Blogging can be a very effective way to generate online interest in your business, particularly if your business website and blog are integrated. Regular blogging, comprising fresh, good-quality content embedded with relevant links, can generate lots of page hits. It can also lead to other bloggers embedding links to you on their sites. This infuses your site with 'link juice' that increases your search engine rankings over time.

A few words of caution: blogging takes up a lot of time and requires commitment if done regularly. Carving out a niche for yourself so that you're not reinventing the wheel takes careful thought. Having an established network is essential if you want to blog effectively. People who read blogs are used to finding the content they're interested in by using the web. If you are not 'connected', how will you let your potential users know that you exist? If you're not using the likes of Facebook, Twitter, LinkedIn or Google+ you may find it harder to generate the initial interest and 'virality' that online social media provide.

Another issue to consider is that in order to work primarily as a work-generation tool, your blog should to be appropriate to the end users of your services, not just your colleagues or friends. It needs to instil a sense of confidence in clients that you understand and care about their needs and concerns, and it should reflect your professional competence.

PRACTITIONER FOCUS

Marcus hosts a blog on his website that is dedicated to helping writers improve their self-editing skills. Independent authors often find their way to him via this medium and he firmly believes that writers come away from reading his blog thinking he's an editor who really cares about, and thinks about, the work he does. Anna blogs about scientific journal publishing, focusing in particular on how to help researchers get their papers submitted. Her posts show academics that she understands the world in which they are working and the publishing challenges they face. These practitioners' blogs attract potential clients to their websites – the content is designed to help the client, so the blogs act as lead-generation tools.

Kate has taken a hybrid approach aimed at the freelance community, clients, writers and students. The content she provides addresses different communities at different times and acts as both a lead- and network-generation tool.

Louise, on the other hand, has built a freelance business-building knowledge centre. Her blog attracts fellow editors and proofreaders – the content is designed to help the colleague, so the blog acts primarily as a network-generation tool. Note, however, that some of her indie author and student clients have told her that even though the content wasn't aimed directly at them, the professional style of her writing gave them confidence in her language abilities and encouraged them to contact her.

Carol Tice, writing for Freelance Switch, sums up the philosophy nicely: 'Think of your blog as simply another portfolio sample of your work. If it shows your skills, it still works, even if the particular topic isn't of interest to your clients' ('Do Freelancers Have to Blog to Get Clients?', Freelance Switch)

The blogging practitioners discussed above don't ultimately think of their blogs in terms of lead- and network-generating tools. They blog because they want to share information with a particular community. I think this is key to successful blogging – do it because you want to and because you enjoy it. The value added to your business is just that, value added, but good content comes from an ongoing passion to share ideas.

7.10 Trade magazines, newsletters and journals

If you are a member of a professional association, because of, say, technical expertise, do you know a magazine, newsletter or journal that you might advertise in? If so, take a look to see how other service providers are using the ad space and make a note of any that you'd like to consider.

7.11 Social media networks

Actually, the term 'social media' doesn't do justice to the opportunities these networks provide. More accurate, for our purposes, is to consider them online business media networks. Use your business plan to consider how you will utilize the likes of Twitter, LinkedIn and Facebook. The degree to which these drive your work stream will depend on how you use them and what you put into them.

Effective utilization is all about sharing – fostering a sense of community and being prepared to promote the work, skills and resources of others as well as promoting yourself. All allow the user to show off core skills, and to a limited extent you can design your space in a way that mirrors your business brand.

Reports from editorial freelancers vary as to how much direct work these profiles generate. LinkedIn is becoming an increasingly important search tool for recruitment agents, business professionals and writers looking for editorial service providers, as one of our practitioners explains in the following example.

PRACTITIONER FOCUS

'It does seem like LinkedIn has finally reached some kind of critical mass,' says Liz. 'Just in the past couple of weeks I've had more leads and firm offers of work from that platform than in the previous five years. It feels like an essential now rather than just an extra.' The message from this is that you'd be daft not to start thinking about your LI pitch – the message you want to sell about the services you offer and your USPs. Use your business plan to think about how you might build your profile as you progress through your editorial freelancing journey.

Many editorial freelancers find that different social media networks work in different ways for them. While not all will be primary drivers of your work stream, the excellent networking opportunities these platforms afford, in combination with the possibility that you might get found by a client, mean it makes sense to take advantage of them. There's no financial outlay, either, so the only costs will be on your time. Your colleagues are there – you should make it your business to be there, too.

 PRACTITIONER FOCUS

Some of the practitioners featured in this guide have direct experience of how online networking led to work referrals.

Louise referred by Marcus: Marcus was approached by an old friend to carry out some onscreen proofreading work for her Barcelona-based translation agency. He wasn't in a position to take on the work and so was asked for recommendations. Marcus didn't know Louise at the time but he was aware, via LinkedIn discussion groups, about her experience with onscreen proofreading; he suggested his friend investigate further. The friend looked at Louise's website and then made contact. The translation agency continues to be a regular client.

Nick referred by Louise: Louise and Nick met through Facebook's extensive editorial network. They shared an interest in the marketing side of freelance work and began to bounce ideas around regarding their respective businesses. Nick also assisted Louise with some technical issues, in particular when content from her website was plagiarized. When Louise was later approached by a prospective business client who needed a proofreader with InDesign experience, she referred the client to Nick, who secured the project and subsequent follow-up work.

7.12 Society job boards

Joining a professional association can be a productive way of promoting your services and gaining access to work that your colleagues (or clients) have posted on membership-only job boards. For example, the following editorial societies have job banks: Society for Editors and Proofreaders (UK); some regional chapters of the Institute of Professional Editors (Australia); Council of Science Editors (transnational); Mediterranean Editors and Translators (transnational); Editors' Association of Canada; Editorial Freelancers Association (US).

Others occasionally post jobs on their online discussion lists, including: Board of Editors in the Life Sciences (transnational); Professional Editors' Group (South Africa); Society of English Native-Speaking Editors (Netherlands).

PRACTITIONER FOCUS

The SfEP's Marketplace forum is an active platform for work referrals and accessible only to members and associates. As of writing, Louise has posted seventeen proofreading jobs there over a five-month period, but she's just one of many who pass on the opportunity to quote for work. Naturally, some of the jobs posted specifically ask for very experienced editorial freelancers but there are often opportunities for newer entrants to the field. Her local group also has a dedicated discussion list and some members prefer to share job opportunities within this more local environment in the first instance. Here, members have met face-to-face and developed deeper friendships. They know what their colleagues' subject specialisms and skill levels are and therefore feel able to target work offers more effectively.

Professional society membership is therefore much more than an opportunity to network and seek advice from fellow freelancers. For new starters it can be a direct line to potential clients. Even if you don't secure the job, it enables you to practise quoting for work and communicating directly with service users.

7.13 Deals/offers

Financial deals and offers are thorny issues in the editorial freelancing world and are not favoured by all freelancers for all client types. However, I mention them because they are an option and it would be disingenuous of me not to acknowledge that some of your colleagues will be using a pricing strategy to generate business.

- Your pricing strategy may include offering special deals to self-publishing authors, discounted rates for students, seasonal offers or time-limited discounts for businesses. Note, though, that many mainstream publishers set their own rates, so this strategy is unlikely to be effective in attracting them.

- If you are targeting small, independent clients who can't afford the standard market rates and usually handle editorial work in-house, you might consider offering lower rates/gratis work initially in order to gain experience.

- You might also run a competition on your website with the prize of a free edit/proofread, BOGOF (buy one get one free) deals, or discounts for clients and any referrals they make.

- You could offer, as standard, a free sample edit/proofread for independent authors so that they can assess your work.

The deal/offer you choose should be carefully thought out. You need to be sure that you are not giving something away for nothing. If you are looking to gain experience and testimonials that count then you need to be making the appropriate offer to the appropriate sector of the market. Be creative, but keep your focus.

7.14 Other ways to use the internet

As I've already said, there are no right or wrong methods when it comes to business promotion. Some of the most effective techniques to getting noticed come from those with the most creative imaginations.

7.14.1 Video

Editorial freelancers are using the internet to broadcast videos of their services. Go to YouTube and enter 'proofreading services' in the search box. Some business owners have chosen to star in their shoots; others have used clients, and still others have gone for a pictorial approach with a voice-over.

PRACTITIONER FOCUS

Nick provides one of my favourite examples of using the internet creatively. He decided to combine the power of the testimonial with video – some of his clients share their experience of Nick's proofreading, copy-editing and copywriting services. Nick's visitors can watch these videos on the Full Proof website but they're also available on YouTube.

7.14.2 Downloadable CVs/brochures

A somewhat less flamboyant idea is the downloadable CV. Having a website is a great space in which to detail the services you offer, but some clients may prefer a one-page summary that they can download and print, particularly if they want to compare a number of different service providers. Remember to present the core elements as discussed at the beginning of the chapter: your USPs, the services your provide, any training relevant to your target client group, experience to date, some glowing praise from a satisfied client and your contact information. Keep the copy tight so that it sits comfortably on one page, and add colour for visual interest.

PRACTITIONER FOCUS

Louise decided to create a PDF summary of her services so that prospective clients could download something to hold on file. Somewhere between a brochure and CV, the one-page leaflet features her business name, a quote from a client, a summary of services, qualifications, formats in which she works, recent clients, a selected list of recent projects and her contact details. Thumbnail book jackets of projects she's completed add visual interest. It's simple but attractive, and the embedded Scribd file on her website generates an average of twenty-five downloads a month (though she acknowledges that some of these are from curious colleagues!).

7.14.3 Online portfolios

Once you start to build up a portfolio of work, you'll want to promote this on your website. There are various approaches you can take. Some editorial freelancers opt for clarity over clutter, providing a selected list of works completed; others, like me, opt for a comprehensive listing; and others use article-style presentation, telling the story of their editorial work past and present. Do what feels comfortable for you and your presentation style.

KEY POINTS

- Use the information you've already considered in your business plan regarding your USPs and your pitch to decide where you will focus the elements of your promotion strategy.

- Build a promotion strategy around multiple tactics, not just one, so that potential clients can find you across a variety of platforms.

- Savvy promotion is about being active (e.g., making direct contact, attending events/meet-ups) as well as passive (e.g., directory listings/website).

- Emphasize what you *can* do for your client, not what you can't.

- Test! See what works and what doesn't. There's no such thing as failure when it comes to marketing, only lessons learned.

- Be creative – you're only limited by your imagination.

- Utilize the power of testimonials to develop a sense of trust with potential clients, whatever your promotional platform.

- Don't forget to network – colleagues are not just competitors; they're friends, too.

8 NETWORKING

Networking is an important part of your business strategy. It allows you to share with and learn from other people who are already doing the job.

Many of us become freelance because it suits our needs – moving house, moving country, redundancy, parenting, disability, and caring for dependents are just some of the reasons why people move their work base from the office to the home. These changes can bring rewards but also challenges, forcing us to withdraw from the traditional and easily accessible friendship and professional groups that we'd previously relied on. Many of us still miss the 'office banter' – the 'colleague' element.

Freelancing can be an isolating experience, and networking puts you in touch with like-minded colleagues – it's your equivalent of the office water cooler!

It's worth taking the time when planning your business to consider how freelancing will affect you, both negatively and positively. That way you can prepare yourself for any downsides and plan for solutions.

8.1 Social media

I surveyed some editorial freelancing colleagues in early 2012. Editorial association-based discussion lists, LinkedIn boards, Twitter and Google+ all came up as recommended spaces for connecting with like-minded colleagues in similar working environments, but Facebook stood out as the place to go to meet, chat, share ideas and let off steam. Facebook is the ultimate freelance water cooler! Using online networking forums means you don't ever have to feel like you're working on our own, even if there's no one else in the room.

PRACTITIONER FOCUS

Although Liz has actively engaged in targeting potential clients in more traditional ways, she has been struck by how powerful social media is as a lead-generation tool. Through LinkedIn, Liz connected with an in-house editor with whom she had been out of touch for some years. This eventually led to the offer of work. Says Liz: 'LinkedIn and Facebook are great for just keeping up casually with contacts and reminding them you exist'. The informal nature of these networks enables Liz to keep others' awareness of her skills, knowledge and experience ticking over, but can be just as useful to the newbie looking to build up contacts over time.

It's not just about creating awareness and the possibility of work, it's about acquiring new knowledge, too, as Marcus reminds us in the following example.

PRACTITIONER FOCUS

Marcus interacts with writers in authors' groups on LinkedIn. He posts his blog series on some of the discussion boards, which has generated further interest in who he is and what he does. Says Marcus: 'You can learn a lot about the author experience, particularly in regard to self-publishing, from reading what writers have to say there, and from talking to them. There are some very perceptive, knowledgeable people on the forums, as well as a few shameless self-promoters, of course, and borderline trolls!'

8.2 Professional organizations

Joining your national editorial freelancing society may be a critical first step to accessing colleagues who face the same professional and personal challenges as you, as well as providing excellent social and learning opportunities. The society may have regular local chapter meetings, an annual conference, workshops, seminars and webinars, mentoring opportunities and discussion lists that you can join. Many have online job boards where you may be able to pick up work, and most have online membership directories that are searched by individuals/organizations looking for editorial freelancers.

PRACTITIONER FOCUS

Kate is an active member of her local SfEP group, which she set up and now co-runs. They meet bimonthly, sometimes for informal socials and sometimes for more organized learning sessions. The meetings have also been used as bridging points between members and local university tutors. Kate and her colleagues have also used 'group power' to bid for large projects that needed the contribution of more than one freelancer. Aside from generating work leads, this kind of professional networking has enabled Kate to share, and learn, fresh ideas about how to run a business effectively. 'All businesses need to evolve and grow, so taking a different view will often bear fruit.'

8.3 Cafe culture

Take yourself off to your local coffee shop for a change of scenery. Even if you're not directly interacting with other people, time spent outside your usual work space is an effective refresher. You can even incorporate your Java time with your work – the cafe may not be the best place in which to do editorial tasks that require deep concentration, but it may be a space where you can catch up on emails, invoicing or any of your more general housekeeping tasks.

8.4 Co-working and work hubs

One of the most innovative solutions is that of the work hub (or shared office). Here, freelancers work alongside each other in an atmosphere that's somewhere between office and the cafe. Work hubs are in their early days, but a good place to start your search in the UK is the Workhubs Network (workhubs.com).

PRACTITIONER FOCUS

Anna has used a work hub for over a year. She believes expanding her editorial business into this kind of shared space has increased her productivity compared with home working. Moreover, 'I've enjoyed having a bit of company in breaks, and I've got some great business tips from other members and from workshops run there'. Some work hubs offer 'co-working days' where others can try the hub for free.

Hubs offer a range of facilities that may include meeting rooms, childcare, IT support, training and seminars.

KEY POINTS

- Many of us need our 'water coolers', online or off, but we can also enjoy the solitude that our freelance homeworking status brings us.

- Think about the kind of person you are. Extroverts may be hit harder by feelings of isolation. Introverts may relish the experience and enjoy the attendant privacy and freedom from interruption.

- Planning ahead will enable you to think about the way you want to organize your time, and space, in a way that suits your personality.

9 PRACTICALITIES AND TOOLS FOR THE JOB

> **Task:** create a list of what hardware, software and tools you'll need to enable you to carry out the practical business of editorial freelancing.
>
> **Learning goal:** to ensure you're prepared to physically do the work.

It's critical that you investigate what kit you'll need for your home office. As stated previously, set-up costs for editorial freelancing are lower than for many businesses, but you'll still need desk space, a comfortable chair, a computer, a phone, an internet connection, various reference books (online or in print), appropriate stationery, relevant software for working on Word files and PDFs, and a website.

You'll need to send invoices, so think about designing a template or using one of the many available online for free. You'll also need a way of tracking any work you carry out, so consider developing a job/tracking accounts template in preparation for when paid work comes in.

There are also a number of tools that can help editorial freelancers work more efficiently and productively. It's worth investigating these and getting used to how they operate before you take on paid work so that you're not faced with any surprises. See the Resources section at the end of the book for useful links.

Planning ahead will mean you can also work out what you need immediately and what you can save up for if money is tight.

9.1 Some ideas to get you thinking ...

A more extensive list of tools (including those listed below) is provided in the Resources section at the end of the guide. Most are free or reasonably priced to suit the budget of the new starter. Here, each of our practitioners lists two of their favourite tools to give you an idea of what's available.

PRACTITIONER FOCUS

Anna chooses: (1) PerfectIt, the consistency checker developed by Intelligent Editing that enables users to maximize quality and enforce a style guide. (2) Two macros, FREdit and SpellAlyse, developed by Paul Beverley, and available in his book, *Macros for Writers and Editors*.

Janet chooses: (1) VMware Fusion to provide a PC platform on her Mac so that she can use PerfectIt. (2) Online subscriptions to *Oxford Reference Pro, Merriam-Webster Collegiate Dictionary*, The Bluebook, and *The Chicago Manual of Style*, all of which enable her to work wherever she might find herself.

Kate chooses: (1) Pilot Frixion erasable pens, available in assorted colours. (2) A large second monitor that can be positioned for both landscape and portrait work, which allows her to compare files easily and scale up portrait images in full.

Liz chooses: (1) Carbonite, automatic online backup software, recommended by Janet (2) Adobe InDesign, a must-have for the highly illustrated books she project manages, which allows her to make last-minute changes to files that are about to go to print.

Louise chooses: (1) The PDF proofreading stamps she created, based on the BS 5261 proofreading symbols, in response to the increasing amount of PDF proofreading she was being asked to do by publishers. (2) Dropbox, cloud-based software that enables users to store, share and transfer files – a great backup tool.

Marcus chooses: (1) Online subscriptions to The Chicago Manual of Style and Merriam-Webster, because he works a lot with American authors. (2) Oxford Dictionaries Pro – free to UK library members, this online resource offers instant access to a range of quality reference titles as well as advice for writers and editors.

Nick chooses: (1) PDF-XChange Viewer, Tracker Software's excellent (and far cheaper) alternative to Acrobat. (2) Office Suite Pro app for Android devices, which allows him to open Word documents on his phone or tablet, calculate word counts, and provide quotes for clients while he's on the move.

KEY POINTS

- Invest your business-planning time in the exploration of, and familiarization with, tools that will improve your productivity and professionalism. You will reap the benefits when you begin working.

- Investigate the myriad free resources available online to make the most of your start-up budget – there are a huge number of freebies available!

- Don't buy expensive tools unless you're sure you'll need them. Most editorial freelancers will need Microsoft Word, but fewer consider Adobe InDesign essential. In the case of the latter, training is advisable, and publisher clients certainly are only likely to let experienced editors loose on their InDesign files!

10 CASE STUDIES – TALES FROM NEW STARTERS

It's all well and good reading the advice from colleagues who've been running their own editorial businesses for years. Indeed, I hope that you've found the information in this guide a useful introduction to how you can think about building your future enterprise. Nevertheless, the world we live and work in is constantly changing. While the choice of many to become freelance has in the past been driven by a desire to have greater control over, and flexibility with regard to, their work lives, the economic downturn that began in 2008 has caused even more people to consider building their own businesses.

So what's it like for new starters operating in this increasingly competitive marketplace? Here, three UK colleagues who have entered the field within the past two years share their stories: what drove them to become editorial freelancers, how they've gained experience and acquired clients, the challenges they've faced on their journeys, and the successes they've started to enjoy. These candid accounts illustrate just how tough it can be, but also show that with determination, honesty and strategic thinking you too can navigate the sometimes bumpy, often rewarding, but never dull world of running your own editorial business.

Mary McCauley

At the time of writing I've been the owner of a proofreading business for one year (not including my amateur days and my professional training). I live in the southeast of Ireland. Having graduated with an honours degree in Marketing, I spent fifteen years working for public bodies in research and business administration. The catalyst for my career change to freelance proofreading was my experience as a co-author and co-editor of our local parish history (published as a community fundraising project).

Setting up a business of any kind can be a little overwhelming so, using my project management experience, I found the best way to approach it was to take things one step at a time, i.e. to set myself business objectives.

The first objective was to obtain an industry-recognized qualification in proofreading: for someone outside of the publishing industry in Ireland, this was a daunting first step. I knew that it was important to gain a recognized professional qualification, not only in order for potential clients to take me seriously but also for my own knowledge and confidence. I wanted to ensure that I was investing my training budget wisely. There were numerous proofreading courses on offer: a key decision was to choose the right one for me. On the advice of the Irish Association of Freelance Editors, Proofreaders and Indexers (AFEPI), I chose the PTC's Basic Proofreading by Distance Learning course. It proved invaluable though very challenging; successfully completing it has given me the confidence to pursue a career in freelance proofreading.

The next objective was to register a business name. In Ireland, if you operate a business under any name other than your own true name, you must register it with the Companies Registration Office (CRO), so this objective was next on my list. I also made contact with the Office of the Revenue Commissioners (Ireland) regarding my tax and VAT status.

Next I set up an office space and office systems. My business background came to the fore here. While it involved the more tedious side of freelancing, it was vital in terms of sending out a clear message, both to myself and my nearest and dearest, that I was taking my business seriously. So I set up a home office space; prepared account spreadsheets to track my income and expenditure; created client spreadsheets to track my client work; determined my charges; designed quotations, invoices, receipts and statements; drafted my terms and conditions; and established a backup procedure for my files.

For security reasons, I did not want to use our family's personal computer so I invested in a new laptop with Microsoft Office software; over the past few months I have built up my suite of editing tools. One of the pleasures of setting up my office has been the creation of my reference library. Good reference books have been essential tools for my work to date and they were a key component of my set-up costs.

The next objective was the exploration and application of business promotion tactics. One of the crucial pieces of advice I read regarding setting up a freelance business was to tell everyone and anyone that will listen about your services. Lest anyone doubt the value of that advice, let me assure you that I discovered it very early on: a neighbour approached me to say that she had just learned that I was a proofreader and had she known this she would have contracted me to work on her self-published book rather than the non-local proofreader she did hire.

I also created Facebook and LinkedIn business profiles. My initial most fruitful online networking was on LinkedIn. I joined shortly after registering my business name and connected with friends and past colleagues. Almost immediately, a former colleague contacted me seeking my proofreading services for her online business. She had learned of my services solely through LinkedIn and has been a regular client ever since.

I also printed business cards and posters, which I delivered by hand to all my local libraries to let the library staff know about my services and my involvement with the local history book (of which the county library had purchased several copies). One simple library visit and chat led to a librarian referring a local author to me – one who subsequently contracted my services. I also displayed posters in local and national colleges and universities. I always carry some business cards with me – you never know when you will need them.

Working from home in rural Ireland, with no previous in-house experience or existing contacts within the publishing industry, was initially quite isolating. Networking online has therefore been very important to me. The Publishing Training Centre, SfEP and Proofreader's Parlour websites were a great resource in the early days and I spent my spare time reading their articles and blogs. This interaction helped to keep me going during the difficult early days and to feel a part of the freelance community.

I've also exploited local networking opportunities. Whilst I had little publishing-industry experience, my fifteen years' administrative and research work involved a lot of business writing, editing and proofreading. The contacts I made from my previous jobs have been of great benefit when seeking commercial proofreading work. The first network I joined was my local Wexford County Enterprise Board network and subsequently the Women in Business Network. I attended one of their local business conferences and found it thoroughly inspiring. More productively, I met the managing editor of a local independent publisher for the first time and this led to a subsequent longer and more informative meeting. As a result I have been introduced to a wider network of media and communications contacts within the Wexford area.

Another core goal was to join professional bodies. One of my primary aims was to establish and run my business in the most professional manner possible and for me this included becoming a member of the relevant professional bodies. Early on, I became an associate of the SfEP and once I had gained more proofreading experience, I became a full member of the AFEPI. I recently attended their AGM in Dublin and, as I didn't know anyone, it was daunting. I am glad that I made the effort, though, as I met some lovely Irish colleagues.

The final objective was to design and publish my own website. The achievement of this goal has been one of the highlights of my first year in formal business. My budget did not stretch to having one designed professionally, yet all the advice indicated the importance of having a website. I decided to design the website myself using Weebly. It was so much easier than I had expected – building the site was nothing compared to having to write the content! Overall, it was a great learning experience.

So where are things now, a year on? I've learned that professional editorial freelancing is hard. In the early days, I had a couple of very promising leads for proofreading work that never came to fruition and this really tested my resolve and self-belief. I used these quiet periods to concentrate on the mechanics of my business, e.g. building my website, networking and reading industry-related material on all aspects of proofreading and freelancing – things not covered in a training-course manual.

My listing in the AFEPI Directory of Members has led to a large increase in the number of enquiries I receive and I have sourced work from some of these. I have also had success in gaining work through the SfEP Marketplace forum and through my website.

Could I make a full-time living of it? At the moment it's definitely just a second income and will be for the foreseeable future. (This is owing to its part-time nature as a result of my parenting responsibilities. Though, if I am working to a tight project deadline, the concept of 'part-time' goes out the window and working early mornings, late nights, weekends and ten-day stretches without a day off becomes the norm.).

I had taken a five-year career break from my local council job in 2006 and during this time (when my three children had all started school) I was invited to work part-time as a (paid) parish secretary. After two years I resigned from that job (June 2012) to concentrate on my proofreading business and to try and make a real go of it before my return-to-the-council-job deadline. Over the past year there have been periods where I've had dry spells. Things have picked up in the past few months. I had nearly a full workload from New Year's Eve up to the start of March 2013 but, even so, it was an agonizing decision to make – whether to return part-time or resign and concentrate on my business. But I've done it – I handed in my notice and have just received my confirmation letter. No more safety net of the secure government job. My nine-year-old said to me, 'But, Mammy, you are a proofreader. Why would you want to go back to your old job? And what would we do with your office in the front room?' Out of the mouths of babes ...

This is a tough business and I am extremely lucky that my family can afford for me to provide only a small second income initially. I am truly blessed that I do not have to hand my children over to a childminder and that I can be their main carer. I am now proceeding with steadily growing my business over the coming years, honing my specialities, continuing to invest in training, upgrading to ordinary membership of the SfEP and positioning myself to become a strong player in the industry in Ireland in the years ahead, once I can dedicate myself full time to it.

Resigning was a leap of faith but I know that I have made the right decision. I've never been happier. I adore my job and I have always wanted to work with words. I know that I am on the right path and that it is onwards and upwards for me, but only because I am completely determined to make it work.

Johanna Robinson

I began the PTC Basic Proofreading by Distance Learning course in December 2011 and received my final assignment back in July 2012. I took the course while I was on maternity leave with our second child. It turns out that I had considered the career years ago: when I moved house in June 2011, I found an old copy of Trevor Horwood's *Freelance Proofreading and Copy-editing*. However, as I had been the family breadwinner for many years, a change of career from lawyer to proofreader had not previously been an option.

When I started, I was very clear that I would focus on one service. I think this comes from having been a lawyer, where general practice is rare these days; a lawyer will usually specialize in one particular area (mine was property). I decided that I would advertise my services as a proofreader. While in reality I have ended up doing a small amount of onscreen editing and a small amount of writing for a regular client, I do not call myself a copy-editor (indeed I would not do so without the relevant training) and certainly not a copywriter. My thoughts are, if someone is looking for a proofreader, they don't want to be distracted by all the other things you offer that they don't want. I think this has worked well in terms of marketing. At present, I love the proofreading, its variety and the relatively quick turnaround it gives me, and I have no immediate plans to train in anything else.

Initially I concentrated on the legal side of proofreading because of my background, although in reality this has only formed a small percentage of the jobs I've done. I have carried out some academic proofreading for a law professor and some subcontracted legal proofreading. However, I have just submitted my application to the SfEP for the legal mentoring programme. My other work has been in a range of genres, for a variety of clients.

I had originally retrained in order to become a solicitor (my BA and MA were in English Literature) and, while I enjoyed the job itself and valued my firm, the demands and stress attached to the job seemed to be getting more intense. Balancing a full-time workload and two children with a husband who worked away most of the time was going to be tough. I used my maternity leave as an opportunity to plan my new career, but this option was far from safe, as my husband had been made redundant during my maternity leave/PTC course. Had he not been able to find a new job, I would have had no choice but to return to work as a solicitor. Had I been able to work as a lawyer part time, I may well have taken this option and built up my proofreading career alongside.

I was well aware that starting my own business and being a proofreader came hand-in-hand, and I did lots of research before and during the PTC course. I would say that I probably spent the same amount of time on the business side as on the study side: for example, the PTC's Successful Editorial Freelancing course, building and writing my website and Facebook/Twitter/LinkedIn pages, designing my stationery/logos, and lots of online research.

Having worked with small businesses as a property solicitor, I knew that investing time and money in a new career or new venture is essential if it is to succeed. Thankfully, the difference was that I didn't need to lease a building – just a desk in the bedroom! But I bought the books I thought I'd need, joined the SfEP, bought my website package, a printer, had posters and business cards printed, and downloaded the software PerfectIt. I still need a reliable computer, and a proper office chair. And an eye test.

I chose the PTC's distance-learning option because all my research told me this was the course most recognized in the industry. As I was coming from a non-publishing background I wasn't ready for the emphasis on publishing in the course, but in fact it made me consider that working for publishers might be an option. Not only did the rigorous course provide me with basic skills, but also the content, training and exercises made me think in a certain way and helped me look out for certain things. I still refer back to my notes frequently.

The PTC's online Successful Editorial Freelancing course contained valuable information and useful short exercises, and I was examined on my business plan. I had never done a business plan before but it was an excellent exercise in focusing my attention on the practicalities of freelancing: the small details and the big picture. I came up with lots of ideas for marketing, some of which I've used and some of which are on the back burner. Some of the course exercises involved setting up spreadsheets for expenses, invoices, etc., so these essential resources were already in place by the time I got my first piece of proofreading work.

I've also attended the SfEP's Proofreading Problems course. It made a change to do face-to-face training, and it is a prerequisite for the mentoring scheme that I've applied for. Ultimately I hope to upgrade from associate to ordinary membership of the SfEP. I'd also like to do the oncreen editing training and a grammar course. The training isn't cheap, but I would strongly recommend that anyone thinking of setting up as a proofreader have a 'training fund' in place before starting, and to look at this as one of the essential expenses involved in starting a new business, particularly if you have no other official experience behind you. You have nothing to invest in if not yourself.

I also have Margaret Aherne's book, *Proofreading Practice*, which I am working through (very) slowly, but which is an excellent, value-for-money resource. I hope to get round to taking non-proofreading courses, such as those provided online by HMRC and Business Link.

Other vital resources are forums: large ones such as the SfEP's and others such as a small online group of editors and proofreaders I am a member of. There is also lots of useful information available if you follow the right people on Twitter.

I received my first job in August 2012 and, as it was a hard-copy proofread (on paper) using the BSI proofreading symbols, it was an excellent starting point. It was a book written by a solicitor on the legal issues surrounding branding, aimed at entrepreneurs. She had set up her own publishing company and is therefore essentially a self-publisher, although she did use a book consulting service. The job was posted on the UK freelance website PeoplePerHour and I got the job because, unlike most freelancers applying for it, I could use the necessary symbols (the document had been copy-edited and typeset) and because I had been a lawyer.

I am aware that such websites can be controversial for various reasons: the quality of the work; the quality of the freelancers; the fact that 'bidding' can drive down prices and hence earnings, not just for the individual but arguably across the board. While I am sure these arguments are often valid, my own experience does not actually bear them out. My first job paid in line with rates often paid by publishers. The client did not choose the lowest bidder, but the person they considered could do the job best. As it was then my only job, I could take the time to do the job well and do it accurately. The lack of feedback is often quoted as a downside to this job. However, I have received good-quality feedback via this medium. While clients may or may not be able to tell the difference between good and bad proofreading (and I think they can), I was fortunate that at the book launch for my first project, a well-known editor of a legal journal complimented me on the proofreading I had done, meaning I could move on to the next job with more confidence.

I have since carried out another job for my first PeoplePerHour client and have had many interesting and decently paid jobs from the site. This is, however, due to various factors: I have a good, concise and well-written profile; I submit accurate and comprehensive bids; I have positive feedback for previous jobs; and I have a PDF CV that I attach to most of my bids. I also pay attention to the quality of the job. I am quite picky about what I bid for. I won't bid for badly paid jobs and I assess the quality of the language in the job posting itself. Now that I am an established freelancer on the site, I am being approached by clients rather than having to bid for work.

I also asked friends and family if they had any ideas for marketing; one suggested offering to proofread law students' training contract applications (she sifts them) and I added this service to my website, which has resulted in a couple of interesting jobs. I contacted everyone I knew who was even vaguely involved in publishing, and while nothing has come of personal contacts so far, my list is still there, so as my skill base increases and CV improves, I can return to those contacts.

While I trained I created my website using MrSite, a company I had used previously for other websites. I set up a Facebook page (which I am very guilty of neglecting) and a Twitter account (marginally less neglected). LinkedIn has all my education, work history and my proofreading-related training and courses; one of my clients has left a lovely, unsolicited recommendation on there. At the outset I created a 'short', leaflet-style CV in PDF format. It lists very basic information and a couple of short testimonials, but it shows, when I email it to a potential client, that this is my job, my business – that I'm not 'dabbling'.

In my previous job as a lawyer I did some face-to-face networking, mainly with women-focused networking groups such as Forward Ladies. I used to find that these kinds of events can be difficult to get work from – but not impossible. There can be some fun things to attend, and interesting people to meet, but I don't really have the time to attend such networking events regularly at present. I have attended one SfEP North West group and hope to attend the Manchester group meeting in future.

I also set up a marketing spreadsheet so I could see exactly what I had done, and when and what the results of my efforts were. Louise Harnby's blog was invaluable in pointing me in the right direction. After finishing my training, I sent emails to a handful of very small local publishers – who wouldn't have had the resources to pay for a proofreader – offering to work for free. In response I had an 'on file', a 'no' and two no-replies. Had I not managed to get some paid work I would, however, have continued down this route. I did some proofreading for a creative writing charity, I proofread for my son's school, and I contacted the National Blind Children's Society as its website said it wanted voluntary proofreaders. (I didn't hear back but would have pursued this by telephone if I had been desperate for experience.)

And I sent Christmas cards to my regular clients ...

There are challenges. At the moment, I have a toddler and a school -age child. My toddler has a lengthy nap in the afternoon so I am able to work at that time. My husband works away for five days at a time and so this allows me to work in the evenings. It's not easy fitting things around the family, but it's a lot less stressful than being a full-time solicitor.

I will say that if we were relying on my income then things would become more stressful. I supported my husband for many years while he trained/looked for work and now the roles are reversed. Having said that, my proofreading is by no means a hobby. The time I spend working is valuable and I want to get paid as much as I can for that time. We need and value the income, and as both children get older I hope to be able to invest more time in my work. Proofreading is a challenging area of work to get into. There are many, many experienced freelancers out there. Work will not fall into your lap. But, if you're well prepared, in a financial and a business sense, have a useful background/former career, and have exceptional client care, it will come together – it might just take time. No one starting a new business would expect it to take off the day it opens its doors – or even some months or years down the line. And when the work does arrive, there can be lots of late nights!

I'm pleased with what I've achieved so far. My jobs have included a YA science-fiction novel (for a self-publisher but professionally copy-edited), a six-monthly design magazine, daily website editing for a commercial property agent, monthly in-flight magazines, a higher-education college brochure, a 100-page travel brochure, a start-up fashion magazine, a self-publisher's crime novel, a paediatric training manual and various other bits and pieces. I have also had some work from Find a Proofreader (especially in September: dissertation month).

Two months after finishing the PTC course and having completed four or five jobs, I was working down my list of 'legal publishers' to contact. I decided to send a couple of emails out at a time: one, briefly listing my experience and background, was to a well-known UK academic publisher. I was surprised that they sent me their test, and more surprised that I passed! A trial project followed a couple of months later and I've now been added to their panel of freelancers. I would love to have a combination of publishing clients, serious self-publishing clients and businesses.

I find that now, I still rely very much on skills that I learned as a lawyer: following a client's brief, attention to detail, client care, and practical IT skills.

Grace Wilson (pseudonym)

My decision to become an editorial freelancer was very much driven by my personal circumstances. I'm a widow and my daughter has learning disabilities. Until a few years ago the two of us had lived together on a package of state benefits related to her needs. When my daughter moved into independent living, her benefits transferred with her. I knew this was coming and had time to prepare, so I completed The Publishing Training Centre's Basic Proofreading by Distance Learning course. I felt that freelance proofreading would suit me because I'd been a full-time single carer for years – the idea of trying to sell the skills necessary for an office environment was, frankly, unthinkable. I've always had a good eye for detail and my written English is good, so editorial freelancing seemed a viable option, and something I could do to supplement my pension later on, too.

Setting up your own business is so tough, though. I had no idea. The thing about this business is that in the early days you have to keep pushing; I'm emotionally very sensitive and prone to depression, so even when I acquired my first few pieces of work, the fact that the rates I was earning in no way reflected the suggested minima advertised by some professional societies made me feel I was failing in some way. Rather than seeing these recent jobs as experience gained, and hooks to sell on to potential new clients, I withdrew. Freelancing can be a lonesome experience but depression can be utterly isolating. I ended up back on state benefits and lost complete faith in my ability to build a proofreading career.

The story of my editorial freelancing journey might have ended there had it not been for the amazing free advice, support and training I received from the staff at the benefits office. In particular, the free business training injected me with a huge dose of fresh determination, and the staff helped me develop a business plan, which then qualified me to get the enterprise allowance. With renewed confidence I set about building my company.

Initially, I relied mainly on word of mouth. That generated some nice references but I wasn't extending my network beyond friends and family. The business tutors encouraged me to attend a business college meeting for new start-ups. There I met other new business owners, including someone who was launching his own website development business. He built my website for a discount and I proofread his web content for the same deal. Extending my network into a community of other business owners taking a similar journey was a good move. We help each other out and promote each other's services. And I've continued to make a point of telling everyone what I do; I'm always waving my business cards around!

Talking with my business tutors helped them to understand what makes me tick, and me to understand how I could use those qualities to find a focus. I decided to target the 'small man on the street' – people like me, my family and friends who want to deal with approachable people who make them feel that they are in safe hands; they want to be stroked. And I'm good at doing that – that's my USP! I created the strapline of 'Customer-friendly proofreading at comfortable prices'. Understanding the kind of editor these types of private client want to work with, and ensuring the message I communicate expresses this, has been really important and helped attract independent writers to my website. Many of my self-publishing clients have told me they feel intimidated and nervous when looking for somebody to tackle their writings, but that I reassured them.

I've also been very targeted regarding my contact with publishers. I decided to get experience by contacting an independent press that specialized in genre fiction – Wildhorse Publishing (name changed for confidentiality). Prior to meeting me, they did all their proofreading and copy-editing in-house. I didn't bother them with unsolicited letters that offered them nothing in return for the boredom of reading them; I carried out a check on one of their books and sent them a friendly list of errors I'd found, ostensibly so that they could maybe correct them for the second edition, but really to show them how marvellous I am! And I was shameless! I made them a financial offer they couldn't refuse, and they gave me a break. I didn't feel bad about this – I wasn't undercutting anyone else in the freelancing marketplace because Wildhorse didn't contract out editorial work. I work on a fixed rate per book and now that I'm familiar with their house style, and we're all clear on the brief, I've managed to improve the amount of money I earn per hour.

If I want to expand my business, the next step is to write to the production editors of fiction publishers and sell on the experience I've gained with Wildhorse. I could probably get better rates (though still way below the SfEP or NUJ's suggested minima) and I think I have enough experience to be able to stand out.

Things I've learned: (1) If I did it all over again, I'd do all the business planning and courses before, or while, I was doing my editorial training, not after. I think this would have given me more confidence in the beginning and prepared me for the reality. I might not then have let things get on top of me to such a degree. (2) I wish I'd been more realistic about what I was going to earn; perhaps I wouldn't have judged myself so harshly. There's nothing wrong with taking small, lower-paid jobs when you're a newbie. These keep the skills that you've learned while training from rusting away in the early days and they give you confidence that you can actually do the work.

11 THE LAST WORD ...

This guide reflects the style of business planning I developed when I began my journey into freelance proofreading in 2005. Your plan may look very different, but the important thing is to have one. Taking the time to think strategically about your experience, strengths, target market and learning opportunities will clarify your purpose, prevent time wastage, and focus your mind on what needs to be done, how you are going to do it, the objectives behind your choices, and the outcomes you aim to achieve.

Setting up a freelance editorial business is not so different from setting up any other business – it's hard work. It will take time and you will need to be enthusiastic, persistent and focused. Anyone who tells you there's plenty of work out there that you'll be able to exploit at the first available opportunity is either misleading you or has been misinformed. There is plenty of work but a large chunk of it is being done by established editorial freelancers who already have their businesses up and running, and who have excellent reputations, lots of references and a wealth of experience. They are the people you'll be competing with. Careful business planning in the early stages is therefore an essential step to success.

I wish you all best with your editorial business-building journey.

Louise Harnby, April 2013

RESOURCES

Editorial freelancing societies and directories (selected)

Most of the editorial societies listed have searchable membership directories.

Australia: **Institute of Professional Editors (IPEd)**; regional chapter links include searchable membership directories: iped-editors.org

Canada: **Editors' Association of Canada (EAC)**: www.editors.ca

Germany: **Verband der Freien Lektorinnen und Lektoren (VFLL)**: www.vfll.de

Ireland: **Association of Freelance Editors, Proofreaders and Indexers (AFEPI)**: www.afepi.ie

Japan: **Society of Writers, Editors and Translators (SWET)**: www.swet.jp

Netherlands: **Society of English Native-Speaking Editors (SENSE)**: www.sense-online.nl

South Africa: **Professional Editors' Group**: www.editors.org.za

Spain: **Asociación Española de Redactores de Textos Médicos (AERTeM)**: www.redactoresmedicos.com

Transnational: **BELS: Board of Editors in the Life Sciences**: www.bels.org

Transnational: **Council of Science Editors (CSE)**: www.councilscienceeditors.org

Transnational: **Eastern Mediterranean Association of Medical Editors (EMAME)**: www.emro.who.int/entity/emame

Transnational: **European Association of Science Editors (EASE)**: www.ease.org.uk

Transnational: **Find a Proofreader** (specialist directory): http://findaproofreader.com

Transnational: **International Society of Managing and Technical Editors (ISMTE)**: www.ismte.org

Transnational: **Mediterranean Editors & Translators (MET)**: www.metmeetings.org

Transnational: **PeoplePerHour**: www.peopleperhour.com

Transnational: **Professional Copywriters Association (PCA)**: www.the-pca.org

UK: **Publishing Training Centre** (specialist training organization with freelance directory): www.train4publishing.co.uk

UK: **Society for Editors and Proofreaders (SfEP)**: www.sfep.org.uk

UK: **Society of Indexers**: www.indexers.org.uk

USA: **American Copy Editors Society (ACES)**: http://stl.copydesk.org

USA: **American Society for Indexing**: www.asindexing.org

USA: **Bay Area Editors' Forum (BAEF)**: www.editorsforum.org

USA: **Copyediting-L**: online discussion group and directory: www.copyediting-l.info

USA: **Editorial Freelancers Association (EFA)**: www.the-efa.org

USA: **Northwest Independent Editors Guild**: www.edsguild.org

USA: **San Diego Professional Editors Network (SD/PEN)**: www.sdpen.com

UK editing/proofreading training providers (selected)

The information provided does not serve as an endorsement (unless otherwise stated) of the services listed. I feel that it's only fair to recommend those providers whom I've used. It is essential you select any training provider, listed here or otherwise, based on your specific business needs. If you live outside the UK, consult your national professional editorial association to find out what training options they recommend. And remember the advice I offered earlier in the guide:

Base your choice of training provider, first and foremost, on the quality of the course – the knowledge you will acquire and the skills you will learn – not on marketing straplines.

RECOMMENDED: **Publishing Training Centre** (note, in particular, their Successful Editorial Freelancing distance learning course, which is an excellent complement to this guide): www.train4publishing.co.uk

RECOMMENDED: **Society for Editors and Proofreaders**: www.sfep.org.uk

Chapterhouse: www.chapterhousepublishing.co.uk

Courseitsme: www.courseitsme.com

CTJT: www.ctjt.biz

Editorial Training: www.edittrain.co.uk

Freelancers.co.uk

Gpuss.com

Harris, N. (1991) *Basic Editing: A Practical Course* (book; only available on the second-hand book market)

Harris, N. (1991) *Basic Editing: The Exercises* (book; only available on the second-hand book market)

London School of Publishing: www.publishing-school.co.uk

Maple Academy: www.emagister.co.uk

Margaret Aherne Editorial Training:
www.meaherne.webeden.co.uk

Open College: www.ukopencollege.co.uk

Publishing Scotland: www.publishingscotland.org

The No-Nonsense Proofreading Course (ebook):
www.proofreading-course.com

The Writers Bureau: www.writersbureau.com

Tools (selected)

About.me: a sharp little platform that enables you to create a one-page website in minutes (free)

Adobe InDesign: desktop publishing software much favoured by publishers, designers, typesetters and businesses preparing ready-for-print material (prices vary; subscription model available)

BrokenLinkCheck: online broken link checker (free):
www.brokenlinkcheck.com

Carbonite: cloud-based automatic online backup tool (prices start at ($59 per year): www.carbonite.com

Chicago Manual of Style Online:
www.chicagomanualofstyle.org

Dropbox: file-transfer and backup tool (2GB free):
https://www.dropbox.com

Editorial job-tracking/accounts template (free):
www.louiseharnbyproofreader.com/4/post/2012/11/editorial-annual-accounts-template-excel.html

EditTools: Rich Adin's suite of Word macros created to improve editors' speed and accuracy ($69; free trial download available):
http://wordsnsync.com/edittools.php

FileZilla: File Transfer Protocol (FTP) software – quick to download and easy to use (free): https://filezilla-project.org

Hewlett-Packard Learning Center (free):
www.hp.com/certification/whats_learning_center.html

Invoice templates: basic invoice templates are available from Microsoft and can be adapted to suit your needs (free):
http://office.microsoft.com/en-gb/templates

Late Payment Interest Calculator (free):
http://late-payment-law.co.uk/calculator.html

Macros for Writers and Editors: Paul Beverley's extensive downloadable book featuring over 400 macros (free)
www.archivepub.co.uk/book.html

Microsoft Office, including Word, Excel, PowerPoint and Publisher (prices vary)

MS Office Training Tutorials (free):
http://office.microsoft.com/en-us/training-FX101782702.aspx

OfficeSuite Pro: MobiSystems' app allows users to view, edit, print and share Word, Excel and PowerPoint files on Android devices while on the move (£9.19):
www.mobisystems.com/android_office

Oxford Dictionaries Pro: including online access to OUP's dictionaries and thesauri, *New Hart's Rules* and *Pocket Fowler's Modern English Usage* (free to UK library members):
http://english.oxforddictionaries.com

Parallels Desktop: allows users to run Windows and Mac applications side by side: http://www.parallels.com/products/desktop

PDF proofreading stamps: Louise Harnby's BS-5261 PDF markup symbols (free): www.louiseharnbyproofreader.com/4/post/2012/08/roundup-pdf-proofreading-stamps-quick-access-links.html

PDF-XChange Viewer: PDF editing software from Tracker Software; alternative to Acrobat (free; pro version $37.50):
www.tracker-software.com/product/pdf-xchange-viewer

PerfectIt ($59; free trial available): www.intelligentediting.com

Pilot Frixion erasable rollerball pens, available in assorted colours (£1.92): www.pilotpen.co.uk

ReferenceChecker (£49.95; free 10-day trial): www.goodcitations.com

Resources for Word users: Liz Broomfield's online, easy-to-understand instructions on how to get the best out of Word (free): http://libroediting.com/?s=resources+for+Word+users#wrd

ShortcutWorld.com: keyboard shortcuts for software including InDesign, Excel and Word (free)

StatCounter: website traffic analysis program (free): http://statcounter.com

TextStat: text analysis and concordance software, but I use it to generate word-frequency lists and eliminate spelling inconsistencies (free): http://neon.niederlandistik.fu-berlin.de/en/textstat

The Editorium: Jack Lyon's macros and add-ins (some resources are free): www.editorium.com

VMware Fusion: conversion software for running Windows programs on a Mac: www.vmware.com

Weebly: web-hosting service with drag-and-drop interface and customizable templates (free and pro versions available): www.weebly.com

WeTransfer: large file-transfer tool with no sign-up necessary (2GB free): https://www.wetransfer.com

WordPress: blogging tool and web-hosting service with plug-in architecture and customizable templates (free): www.wordpress.com

WordTips: Allen Wyatt's tricks, tips and ideas on how to make the most of Microsoft Word (free): http://word.tips.net/ci.html

Blogs and knowledge centres (selected)

An American Editor: editing and business advice from Rich Adin: http://americaneditor.wordpress.com

Armed with Pens: advice for editors and writers: www.armedwithpens.com

Beyond Paper Editing: tips for writers and editors alike: http://beyondpaperediting.weebly.com

Commas, Characters and Crime Scenes: advice from the front line of fiction editing: http://marcustrowereditor.com

Copyediting.com: editing and language blog

Copyeditors' Knowledge Base: editorial resource centre curated by Katharine O'Moore-Klopf: www.kokedit.com/ckb.php

DCBLOG: David Crystal – writer, editor, lecturer, broadcaster: http://david-crystal.blogspot.co.uk

Editing Mechanics: Hazel Harris's blog 'about how people work together to create great text': http://wordstitch.co.uk/blog/?cat=6

Editorial Inspirations: editing and proofreading blog from April Michelle Davis: www.editorialinspirations.com

EditorMom: editing, medical editing and business aspects of freelancing: editor-mom.blogspot.com

Freelance Feast: Meg E. Cox shares ideas about working independently in healthy ways: www.freelancefeast.com

Freelance Folder: freelance tools, resources, tips and advice: http://freelancefolder.com

Freelance Switch: sound practical advice on freelancing: http://freelanceswitch.com

Grammar Girl: Mignon Fogarty's Quick and Dirty Tips: http://grammar.quickanddirtytips.com

Kateproof blog: covers all things proofreading and editing: www.kateproof.co.uk/blog

LibroEditing blog: editorial freelancing business and grammar tips from Liz Broomfield: http://libroediting.com/blog

Lingua Franca: language and writing blog from *The Chronicle of Higher Education*: http://chronicle.com/blogs/linguafranca

PublishEd Adelaide: a blog for editors, publishers, authors and anyone who works with words: http://publishedadelaide.com.au

Publishing Training Centre blog: freelancing, publishing knowledge base and grammar tips: www.train4publishing.co.uk/blogs

Sentence First: Stan Carey's English-language blog: http://stancarey.wordpress.com

Sharmanedit: Anna Sharman's journal publishing blog with a focus on biomedical science: http://sharmanedit.wordpress.com

Subversive Copy Editor: advice from Chicago: www.subversivecopyeditor.com

The Editor's POV: forum for freelance editors of fiction: http://theeditorspov.blogspot.com

The Proofreader's Parlour: Louise Harnby's resources, tips and knowledge sharing related to the business of editorial freelancing: www.louiseharnbyproofreader.com/blog.html

Without Exception: Beth Cox blogs about inclusion and editing: www.withoutexception.co.uk/blog.php

Writers and Editors: Pat McNees on writing, editing and publishing: www.writersandeditors.com/blog.htm

Books and online reference materials (selected)

Aherne, M., (2011) *Proofreading Practice: A Book of Exercises with Model Answers and Commentary* (Improving Books; available only from Aherne's website)

Baxter, P., *Theses and Dissertations: Checking the Language* (SfEP Guides)

Burchfield, R. W. (2004) *Fowler's Modern English Usage*, re-revised 3rd ed. (Cambridge University Press)

Butcher, J., Drake, C. and Leach, M. (2006) *Butcher's Copy-editing: The Cambridge Handbook for Editors, Copy-editors and Proofreaders* (Cambridge University Press)

Cambridge Dictionaries Online: http://dictionary.cambridge.org/

Carr, S., *Editing into Plain Language: Working for Non-publishers* (SfEP Guides)

Harris, N. (1991) *Basic Editing: A Practical Course* (Publishing Training Centre; only available on the second-hand book market)

Harris, N. (1991) *Basic Editing: The Exercises* (Publishing Training Centre; only available on the second-hand book market)

Horwood, T. (1995) *Freelance Proofreading and Copy-editing: A Guide* (ActionPrint Press)

MacMillan Dictionary (online): www.macmillandictionary.com

Merriam-Webster Online: www.merriam-webster.com

Olsen, I., *Editing Fiction: A Short Introduction* (SfEP Guides)

O'Moore-Klopf, K., *Getting Started as a Freelance Copyeditor*: www.kokedit.com/library_booklets.php

Oxford Dictionaries Pro (online): http://english.oxforddictionaries.com

Oxford University Press (2005) *New Oxford Dictionary for Writers and Editors: The Essential A–Z Guide to the Written Word* (Oxford University Press)

Rice, V., *Starting Out: Setting Up a Small Business* (SfEP Guides)

Ritter, R. M., (2005) *New Hart's Rules: The Handbook of Style for Writers and Editors* (Oxford University Press)

The Chicago Manual of Style Online: http://www.chicagomanualofstyle.org/home.html

Trask, R. L. (1997) *The Penguin Guide to Punctuation* (Penguin)

Trask, R. L. (2000) *The Penguin Dictionary of English Grammar* (Penguin)

Waddingham, A., *Editor and Client: Building a Professional Relationship* (SfEP Guides)

Waite, M., ed. (2005) *New Oxford Spelling Dictionary: The Writers' and Editors' Guide to Spelling and Word Division* (Oxford University Press)

Ward, L. J. and Woods, G. (2010) *English Grammar for Dummies* (John Wiley)

Writers' & Artists' Yearbook 2013 (2012) (A & C Black Publishers)

Language editing agencies (selected)

American Journal Experts: www.journalexperts.com

Biodila: www.biodila.com

Bioedit: www.bioedit.co.uk

Biomedical Editing International: www.biomedicalediting.com/

Bioscience Editing Solutions: www.bioscienceeditingsolutions.com

BioScience Writers: www.biosciencewriters.com/EditingJobs.aspx

Cambridge Language Consultants: www.camlang.com

Edanz: www.edanzediting.com

Editage: www.editage.com

Enago: www.enago.com

Genedits: www.genedits.com

Global Edico Services: www.globaledico.com

Oxford Science Editing: www.oxfordscienceediting.com

OxTERMS: www.oxterms.com

SciTechEdit International: www.scitechedit.com/en/home

Scribendi: www.scribendi.com

The Charlesworth Group Author Services: www.charlesworthauthorservices.com

Write Science Right: www.writescienceright.com

Miscellaneous

Business.gov.au: Australian government business advice: http://www.business.gov.au/Pages/default.aspx

CurrencyFair: a peer-to-peer marketplace that allows you to exchange and send funds in a wide variety of currencies: www.currencyfair.com

FreeIndex: UK free ads directory: www.freeindex.co.uk

HMRC's Specific deductions: use of home: examples is a super link for UK editorial freelancers who fill in their own self-assessment forms and want some guidance on what deductions they can include: www.hmrc.gov.uk/manuals/bimmanual/bim47820.htm

HMRC Starting a business: business and tax advice and tutorials for new business owners: www.hmrc.gov.uk/startingup

HotUKDeals: online community of users sharing deals and discount information: www.hotukdeals.com

IRS: Starting a Business:
http://www.irs.gov/Businesses/Small-Businesses-&-Self-Employed/Starting-a-Business

Service Canada: Starting a Business:
http://www.servicecanada.gc.ca/eng/subjects/business

Successful Editorial Freelancing: distance learning course designed to provide students with the practical nuts and bolts of what is required to set up as freelancer in the publishing industry (The Publishing Training Centre): www.train4publishing.co.uk/courses/distance-learning/successful-editorial-freelancing

Starting your own business: advice and video tutorials from GOV.UK

YouTube: one example of a Full Proof video testimonial:
www.youtube.com/watch?v=tzo9H_Ccpsk

Workhubs Network: www.workhubs.com

7463134R00069

Made in the USA
San Bernardino, CA
05 January 2014